Civil War SOLDIERS *of* GREATER CLEVELAND

Civil War SOLDIERS *of* GREATER CLEVELAND

LETTERS HOME TO CUYAHOGA COUNTY

DALE THOMAS

THE History PRESS

Published by The History Press
Charleston, SC 29403
www.historypress.net

First published 2013

Manufactured in the United States

ISBN 978.1.62619.088.7

Library of Congress CIP data applied for.

Contents

Acknowledgements

The Olmsted Historical Society's archives made this book possible with its collection of letters, diaries and images. Lea Thomas proofread the manuscript and offered suggestions. She also supervised the transcription of the diaries written by Amelia Ames and Sabrina Frost Beach and the letters of Sam Ames, Margaret Campbell, Mary Romp, Jonas Franklin Rice, George Kennedy and Elias Hawkins. The transcribers were SITES (Social Involvement Through Education and Service) students from North Olmsted High School: Michael Lee, Catherine Brunner, Shannon Kynion and Eric Marquard.

William C. Stark's excellent history of the 103rd Ohio Infantry Regiment became an essential resource during the writing of this book. In addition, Stark answered numerous questions and read an early draft of the manuscript. Geoffrey and Scot Thomas assisted with their knowledge of computer hardware and software. Geoffrey Thomas also helped with the taking of photographs. Andrew Badalamenti offered comments on the book's introduction. Chris Whipple supplied information about his ancestor, Michael Houck, and contributed images. His father, John G. Whipple, transcribed the letters of Nathan Hawkins and other soldiers of the 103rd Ohio Volunteer Infantry. Lucy McBean, granddaughter of Nathan and Lucy Hawkins, donated these letters to the Olmsted Historical Society. Claude and Carol McBean gave a perspective on the descendants of Nathan and Lucy Hawkins. Gary Porter of the Olmsted Historical Society answered questions about burials in Butternut Ridge Cemetery.

Bob Lamb of the Olmsted Historical Society provided information on Civil War reenactors.

The following persons and institutions also assisted the author: Deborah Shell and Sharon Guinaugh of the Fairview Park Historical Society; Mel Maurer and Lysa Stanton of the Westlake Historical Society; Dan Hill, superintendent of Chestnut Grove Cemetery; the Cuyahoga County Solders' and Sailors' Monument website; the Sons of Union Veterans of the Civil War website; the National Park Service Civil War Soldiers and Sailors System website; the 103rd Ohio Volunteer Infantry Museum and Library (Sheffield Lake, OH); the Westlake Porter Public Library; and the North Olmsted and Fairview Park Branches of the Cuyahoga County Public Library.

INTRODUCTION

The Cuyahoga County Soldiers' and Sailors' Monument on Cleveland's Public Square is a silent reminder of the tragic years of the Civil War. The bronze statues of *The Color Guard*, *At Short Range*, *Mortar Practice* and *The Advance Guard* are frozen in time and usually ignored by busy pedestrians. Hidden from the bustle of the twenty-first century, an interior bronze relief portrays Lincoln emancipating and arming a slave, while the names on the walls give testimony to the war's sacrifices. Few know the monument is located near the site where 100,000 mourners viewed Abraham Lincoln's remains in April 1865.

On the eve of the Civil War, Cleveland had become the commercial center of the Western Reserve. The war hastened this trend with an increase in population and industry. During these years, the population grew by 50 percent, and manufacturing jobs more than doubled. Local businessmen like John D. Rockefeller profited in commercial trading, which led to investments in oil and other industries after the war. In the rest of Cuyahoga County, farming communities generally shared in the prosperity, supplying the agricultural needs of Cleveland. However, the farmers and merchants who went to war caused hardships for their families.

In the first year of the war, four temporary military camps (Taylor, Wood, Brown and Todd) trained volunteers in Cleveland along today's Woodland Avenue from East Twenty-second Street to East Fifty-fifth Street. In July 1862, Camp Cleveland replaced Camp Wade on thirty-five acres of land between West Fifth and West Seventh Streets in the present Tremont region of the city. The camp trained fifteen thousand soldiers, and eleven thousand mustered out there at the end of the Civil War. The barracks, hospital and prison were razed when the camp closed in October 1865.

The women on the home front also did their duty for the Union. From 1861 to 1868, the Soldiers' Aid Society of Cleveland operated out of its location north of St. Clair on Bank Street (West Sixth Street). Primarily funded by private donations, the society cared for the sick and wounded, collected medical supplies and clothing and sent food to troops in the field. The Northern Ohio Sanitary Fair in 1864 raised over $100,000 to finance the society. After the war, veterans received help with finding jobs and applying for government benefits.

Thousands of men in dozens of regiments from Greater Cleveland served in the war. Nathan Hawkins and his brothers-in-law, Frank Campbell and Willie Romp, enlisted in the 103rd Infantry. A friend and neighbor, Sam Ames served in the 124th Infantry. In late summer of 1862, the regiments had organized at Camp Cleveland before leaving for the front.

In 1863, the 103rd Infantry fought skirmish battles in Kentucky before defeating Confederate forces during the siege of Knoxville, Tennessee. Later in the war, the regiment saw considerable action in the Atlanta and Nashville campaigns. The 124th Infantry took part in the fighting at Chickamauga and Chattanooga in 1863 and then the Atlanta Campaign during the following year. In the closing months of the war, the regiment fought in Tennessee at Franklin and Nashville. Both regiments mustered out of service in June 1865. The deaths from combat and disease totaled 458 out of some 2,000 soldiers who had first marched at Camp Cleveland in 1862.

Chapter 1

HOMETOWN

Nathan W. Hawkins was born in June 1832 on his father's farm near Kirtland, Ohio. The youngest son of Russell and Sally Hawkins of Derby, Connecticut, Nathan's maternal grandfather, John L. Tomlinson, had been a captain in the Revolutionary War. Tomlinson received a military land grant in Connecticut's Western Reserve and gave a portion of it to his son-in-law and daughter. After selling the land in 1834, Russell Hawkins moved his family to western Cuyahoga County, where he had purchased a one-hundred-acre farm in southwestern Rockport Township (present-day Fairview Park.) The Hawkins had seven children, three of whom (Caroline, Elizabeth and John) died within eighteen months of their mother's death in January 1843. Soon afterwards, Russell Hawkins married Lydia Foster, a native of Massachusetts.[1]

Nathan's older brother, Russell T. Hawkins, the adventurer in the family, would later go to California.[2] In March 1845, he sent a letter from Wisconsin to Sarah Tomlinson, a cousin living in Rockport, writing, "I am in Prairie du Chien. I came in on business for the Department and shall go out tomorrow. Health is good, money plenty and friends enough." He asked if she had heard from his brother, Eli Hawkins. "Tell me how our stepmother [Lydia Hawkins] gets on and how she crosses the [Rocky] River." He also asked about their mutual friend, a college student. "Tell me how Samantha Palmer is [and] if she is yet at Oberlin."[3] Besides being the first coeducational college in the nation, Oberlin was also a hotbed of antislavery agitation.

The Olmsted Historical Society moved this church to Frostville in 2005. Most likely, the former Wesleyan church served as a stop on the Underground Railroad. *Author's collection.*

Lewis Tomlinson, Sarah's father, used his Rockport homestead in the 1840s as a station on the Underground Railroad. Seeking freedom in Canada, runaway slaves either came through Oberlin or Berea. Although the Western Reserve was mostly opposed to slavery, few were active abolitionists. Tomlinson was a Congregationalist, a group divided over the question of whether a good Christian should violate an unjust law, the Fugitive Slave Act, or work to repeal it. A Sunday school teacher, Tomlinson was a Whig but voted for the Liberty Party in 1848 and the Free Soil Party four years later. Both parties opposed extending slavery into the western territories. He later moved to Carroll County, Illinois, and became a Republican.[4]

A Congregationalist like his brother-in-law, Russell Hawkins also became active in the Underground Railroad. The Hawkins farm was located on a road that ran from Oberlin to the docks of Cleveland (Route 10), a distance of some thirty-five miles. According to his granddaughter, he once "dressed an escaping slave in my grandmother's cape and bonnet for a disguise. She reluctantly loaned it and refused to ever wear the same again."[5] Lydia Hawkins may have been an influence on her stepson, Nathan, who did not become an abolitionist until serving in the Union army.[6]

Nathan did well in school, especially in reading and writing, as his letters later indicated. Years later, he recalled a description of Napoleon crossing the Alps.[7] Among the happier memories of his youth, Nathan remembered in particular celebrating the Fourth of July and later courting his future wife, Lucy Romp:

Nathan Hawkins looked confidently at the camera in 1854. Hawkins's future seemed to be preordained as a Rockport farmer supporting his wife and children. *Olmsted Historical Society.*

> *One does not know when at the age of ten or fifteen what he is going to do in his lifetime, but at that age, his or her happiest is then. The Fourth is spent by him perhaps in eating candies, shooting firecrackers and maybe hunting game in the woods. At any rate, he must burn some powder, or there would be no Fourth of July for him. But now that he is grown up…you will see him washing his buggy and harness, fixing to take a ride through the country, taking with him of course, the girl he likes the best.*[8]

Lucy Romp lived a few miles from the Hawkins farm in Olmsted Township. William Romp, her father, owned a general store and hotel at the top of Cedar Point Road overlooking the Rocky River Valley. The prosperous merchant from New York was also township treasurer for a number of years.[9] In the early 1830s, he had married Anna Frost, eldest daughter of Elias Frost, postmaster and farmer, who lived less than a mile down the road on Kennedy Ridge. Unlike his son-in-law, Frost was a man of limited means without enough land to share with his four sons, three of whom settled in Iowa Territory.

* * *

In the autumn of 1843, Elias and Phoebe Frost went to Iowa after the death of their son. Within a year, Elias died, and although pregnant, Anna Romp joined her mother. Sabrina Frost, a younger sister, helped William Romp take care of the children until he also left for Iowa after hearing his wife had given birth to a son, Willie. The eldest of three daughters, Lucy Romp was thirteen years old at the time and only six years younger than Aunt Sabrina. ("Lucy is half an inch taller than I am and quite slim.") They all came down with chicken pox. The children were soon well again, but their aunt remained sick with "a dreadful pain" in her teeth and ears. In a letter to Iowa, Sabrina longed to have Anna and William Romp return home. Her brother-in-law's mother had "told around town that I have moped about all the time and haint half earned my board. I have stayed here 7 months and did the best I could do." Lucy missed everyone and "sends her love."[10]

Sabrina thought of moving to Iowa if the Frost farm in Olmsted were sold as William Romp advised. "The most I can ask for is to see Father's and Lyman's graves, but I don't never expect to. I never expect to see any other country but this."[11] A year later, Sabrina lost another brother in Iowa. She left Olmsted and then returned with her mother and an orphaned nephew, Francis. They moved back to the Frost farm, where her brother, Elias Frost Jr., lived with his family.

Although not necessarily welcomed by her brother-in-law, Sabrina often visited the Romp household. One stormy day, she received a note from Lucy that was delivered by a customer from the store as he was passing by the Frost farm. "Mother has got some sewing. She would like to have you come and show her something about it if you can. Come and stay a day or two if you can. It may be your luck to see some one that is coming this way that will let you ride."[12]

Lucy and Sabrina were constantly together. Sewing and doing housework, her aunt often worked for the Ames family, who lived west of the Romps on Butternut Ridge next to the cemetery. "We cleaned house all day. That night, Lucy Romp came and stayed with me." It was the spring of 1853, and "the peach trees were all in blossom." Two months later, Lucy told Sabrina of her engagement to Nathan Hawkins.[13] Lucy had first seen Nathan while working in her father's store. She was attracted to the customer with the hazel eyes, dark hair and dark complexion. At five feet nine inches, he stood taller than the average height for those times.[14] They scheduled the wedding for late autumn. On the first day of December, Sabrina went with Lucy to see Henrietta Jones, who cut out the wedding dress:

> *We stayed in the evening. When we went home, it snowed very hard. Saturday, Anna* [Romp] *was sick. I sat up till twelve o'clock* [midnight]

Nathan Hawkins built this house in 1853. Today, a car wash occupies the site at the corner of Lorain Avenue and West 210th Street in Fairview Park. *Fairview Park Historical Society.*

> *sewing. Lucy had been to work in the kitchen. The family was all in bed except Lucy, Mag* [Romp], *and me. Mag and I got us some supper while Lucy mopped the floor. We had a first-rate time eating supper and drinking coffee. When we went to bed, it was two o'clock Sunday.*[15]

Sabrina finished Lucy's dress three days later and then worked on another one for Mag Romp. "Wednesday the 7th in the afternoon, Lucy was married. There was a large company there [in the hall above the Romp Tavern] and dancing in the evening, a fun party."[16] The Reverend J.R. Henry conducted the ceremony. Lucy wore a white silk dress with a bridal bonnet for her marriage vows, later changing into a blue-and-white silk brocade dress for the evening gathering. The groom had a black silk hat for the ceremony and a white one for the reception. Nathan was the last son still living with his parents, and the newlyweds moved into the house he had recently built on his father's farm.[17]

These were happy times for Nathan and Lucy Hawkins. The peace of the decade's first half had resulted from the Compromise of 1850, which kept the nation together in an uneasy truce after the Mexican War. California entered the Union as a free state, and the settlers in the rest of the land taken from Mexico would decide on the question of slavery at the time of statehood. A stronger Fugitive Slave Law was also a part of the omnibus legislation, but storm clouds were soon again on the horizon.

The passage of the Kansas-Nebraska Act in 1854 by a coalition of Democrats and southern Whigs broke the truce. Antislavery northerners felt betrayed because the unorganized region of the former Louisiana Purchase, once closed to slavery under the Missouri Compromise, was now an option if the settlers voted for it. The Whig Party split into two factions, as proslavery southerners fled to the Democrat Party and antislavery northerners formed the Republican Party. Opposition to the Kansas-Nebraska Act was especially strong in Ohio. In the election of 1854, a coalition of voters won all of the congressional districts, and the following year, Salmon P. Chase became Ohio's first Republican governor. In the meantime, popular sovereignty would supposedly lead to a peaceful settlement of the situation in Kansas. Settlers from the North and South began to flow into Kansas Territory.

Lucy Hawkins posed with Libbie in 1855. Her grandfather, Elias Frost, had been the postmaster for Olmsted Township. He named his post office Frostville. *Olmsted Historical Society.*

Ordinary life above the Rocky River Valley, however, took precedence over the growing national crisis. Pregnant and homesick, Lucy wanted to be close to her mother until she gave birth. Nathan agreed, perhaps reluctantly, and the couple moved in with her parents. Now he spent time working on his father-in-law's farm instead of the farm in Rockport. As usual, Sabrina was a frequent visitor. After a Sunday breakfast, "Nate went to salt the cattle, so Lucy and I went with him for a walk."[18]

When the first snow of the season fell in November 1854, Nathan and Lucy were still living in the Romp household. On the last Sunday of the month, Sabrina went to religious services at the schoolhouse next to the Frost farm. "I heard there that Lucy Hawkins was sick. After meeting, I went to see her. She got a baby [Libbie]. It was sick too, and Anna [Romp] wanted me to stay with them all night. I did so." During the following weeks, Sabrina continued to spend time at the Romp home, helping to take care of her niece. On the day before Lucy's twenty-fourth birthday, "I rode with Mr. [Sam] Ames' folks up to Anna's to see Lucy. I found her not as well. I stayed till after tea."[19]

Lucy and Libbie were not well until after Christmas. A month later, Lucy was able to go with her mother to Cleveland while Sabrina took care of the baby. By early February, the time had come for the Hawkins family to return to their house on the Rockport farm. "Lucy moved, and Mag went with her. They called to have me go up and stay with their mother…[who] was so lonesome I went and stayed the afternoon with Anna."[20]

* * *

In early spring, Lucy heard from Sabrina that Uncle Elias Frost Jr. "was calculating to start for Nebraska [–Kansas Territory] in about a week." He planned to vote against the spread of slavery. Fearing for his safety, Sabrina "had a hard cry about it," but having read *Uncle Tom's Cabin*, she understood her brother's motivation. Family qualms seemed to be reflected by the weather. "There was a hard thunder shower that night. The next day, the river was very high…[Mag and Sabrina] went down to the bridge to see the flood wood go over the [gristmill] dam." Lucy heard that Sabrina had decided "to help fix Elias for Nebraska. I made him four collars, a pair of pants and a pair of overalls."[21]

John Kirk and Davis Webster decided to join Frost. They lived down Mastick Road near Joseph Peake, an African American who hid runaway slaves on his farm.[22] On April 25, 1855, the three Olmsted men took the train for Kansas but arrived after the election for the territorial legislature. The voting was plagued by fraud and violence on both sides. However, Kansas quickly organized with a proslavery legislature. What could not be determined by a fair election would soon erupt into a bloody civil war. To the relief of

Although opposed to slavery, Elias Frost Jr. did not volunteer for the Union army because of his age and the large family he had to support. *Olmsted Historical Society.*

his family, Elias returned home in time to celebrate his thirty-fourth birthday.[23]

The cool and wet summer of 1855 turned out to be an unhealthy season in Ohio. On a Sunday afternoon in July, Nathan and Lucy paid a visit to Sabrina. "They came after me. Lucy had a lame foot." She went home with them, washing and ironing for the next two days. On Wednesday afternoon, Lucy's foot improved, but word arrived that Anna and Mag Romp were sick. They took Sabrina to the Romps and "left me with her folks and went home." Not feeling well herself, she took care of them until the Hawkinses returned and stayed overnight with them.[24]

The following week, Nathan and Lucy again needed Sabrina's help, as Libbie had fallen ill with a fever. During her stay, Sabrina found time to do a favor for her nephew's stepmother. "In the afternoon, I cut a dress for old Mrs. Hawkins." Sabrina and Lucy washed the next day, and on Wednesday, "the baby was quite sick. I worked very hard after tea." Then, the following day, Sabrina "was most sick [but] Friday I cut and made the baby a dress. She was quite smart." The next day, "Nathan and Lucy went to her father's [and] I went home with them."[25]

Two months later, the Hawkins family ate Thanksgiving dinner with Sabrina at her neighbor's home in Olmsted Township. In early December, Nathan hitched his horse to a carriage and then took Sabrina and his mother-in-law for a long-promised trip to Cleveland. "It rained all day. It had been uncommonly warm and pleasant…until that day."[26]

* * *

On Christmas Day 1855, Nathan, Lucy and Libbie Hawkins celebrated the season at the Romps' residence at the top of Cedar Point Hill. Presents were exchanged among friends and relatives, and then everyone sat down to a festive meal with William and Anna Romp presiding. Snow started to fall in the afternoon, turning into a blizzard by evening. All the guests stayed overnight. Two days later, Sabrina joined a group of holiday revelers from Olmsted, who "all went down to Nathan's for a visit." They took Mastick Road, which overlooked the drifted snow in the valley. "It was beautiful sleighing…we had a good visit."[27]

The wedding of Mag Romp and Frank Campbell added to the merriment of New Year's Day. The ceremony took place at Mr. Henry's home. Nathan, Lucy and Sabrina stood up for the bride and groom. "When they were married, the company then all came back to Anna's and took supper and then went to Cleveland. Lucy left her babe with Anna, and I stayed and helped take care of her. New Year's Day was very pleasant all day."[28]

A week later, William Romp decided to move his wife and family to Olmsted Falls. "He was so mad because Mag got married. He as good as turned her out of her dowry and forbade the [Campbell] family getting anything out of the store unless it was charged. He was so afraid that Anna would get something to give to Mag. He put his brother into the store."[29]

Mag Campbell's determination to do what she wanted regardless of her father's wishes could be traced back to her student days at Oberlin.[30] William Romp, a conservative Democrat, was the antithesis of the political and social values his daughter learned at the liberal college. In near-zero temperatures, Mag went to see Lucy to discuss her frustrations with their father. Concerned about his wife, Frank Campbell picked up Sabrina on the way to the Hawkins farm. He brought Mag back to Olmsted, and the following week, Sabrina helped them move her things into the home of Frank's parents.

Nathan was not any fonder of his father-in-law than Frank Campbell. While in the army, he wrote a letter to Lucy about an earlier transaction:

> *You said your father wanted some potatoes. I wonder if he ever gave me credit for the potatoes at the time Frank lived up there. He took some to him, and so did I. Also paid him some money on book act* [accounts]. *I* [would] *have Mary* [Romp] *look over his old books and see.*[31]

In the middle of January, the Hawkinses and Campbells surprised Sabrina with a visit on the night before her birthday. Undoubtedly, the conversation included William and Anna Romp's departure to the southern part of the township. Thinking it inferior to Rockport, Nathan did not particularly like Olmsted Falls. A few weeks later without the Campbells, they rode up "to the Falls to see Anna in her new home. [Then] Nathan and Lucy and Anna's hired girl went to a party."[32]

In early May, Lucy visited her ailing grandmother, who was being nursed by Sabrina. Phoebe Frost had been sick and bedridden for a number of weeks, and her daughter was almost always there to help. "It rained most all day. About ten o'clock [in the morning], mother was taken worst. Her feet and hands got cold. She died about nine o'clock in the evening [Friday, May 9]." Sabrina called on John Ames, the local undertaker, to make the coffin and prepare the grave in Butternut Ridge Cemetery. Funeral service took place on Sunday at the Universalist Church.[33]

During one of her visits with Nathan and Lucy, Sabrina may have told them about Henry Beach wanting to marry her. Beach lived with his elderly mother in nearby Dover Township. Unlike the last weddings, there would be no invitations. "Tuesday [June] 25th it was pleasant all day till evening, and then there was a thunder shower. Henry Beach and I went to Esq. Ingerham and were married. We got some wet. I went home with H. Beach that night."[34]

On Thanksgiving Day, Anna Romp invited "Nathan and Lucy, Frank and Mag, Elias and Francis, and the children, and Henry and myself [Sabrina]. We had a first rate supper."[35] The family gathering took place two weeks after James Buchanan had been elected president. The Democrat had won the 1856 election on a platform supporting the Compromise of 1850 and the Kansas-Nebraska Act. He defeated John C. Fremont, candidate of the new Republican Party, who favored the admission of Kansas as a Free State and Congressional authority to decide the status of slavery in the territories. How this election would affect the future of the Union and the lives of those seated around the dinner table may have been discussed that day in late November.

A month later, Lucy Hawkins gave birth to another daughter, Carrie. Hoping his father would give him a part of the farm, Nathan had been raising cows, sheep and hogs in addition to growing wheat, oats, corn and potatoes. The orchard included apple and peach trees. Nathan wanted to build a shed over his well but had never gotten around to it.[36] Over in Olmsted Township, Frank and Mag Campbell were now living in a house on the farm of Elias Frost Jr., where Sabrina had lived while taking care of their mother. Up the road, O.C. Lawrence, a township trustee, now owned the former Romp tavern and general store.[37]

* * *

In April, Nathan received a letter from his cousin Harriet Tomlinson, who lived near Mount Carroll, Illinois. "Where has your brother Eli settled? We have not heard from him since he was here." Harriet had heard they were living in a new house. "We received a likeness of your Lucy and should have expressed our thanks before this." She wondered about the changes in Rockport since they had left for Illinois. Carroll County, like the rest of northern Illinois, was strongly antislavery and Republican like the Tomlinson family. "The Kansas fever rages some here, there are a number going from Mt. Carroll this spring to make claims."[38] By now, Free Soil settlers outnumbered those who favored slavery, but Kansas's statehood was being stalled in Congress by southerners.

Less than thirty miles from Mount Carroll, Freeport became the setting for one of the debates during the 1858 Illinois Senatorial campaign. Stephan Douglas, the incumbent Democrat who had sponsored the Kansas-Nebraska Act, opposed Abraham Lincoln, the Republican challenger. Lincoln dared Douglas to choose between popular sovereignty and the Dred Scott decision of the Supreme Court. (Congress could not interfere with slavery in the territories.) Douglas proposed his so-called Freeport Doctrine. (Prior to statehood, Free Soil settlers in a territory could discourage slavery by refusing to pass laws protecting it.) Douglas won the election but would lose Southern support for his presidential nomination in 1860. Lincoln became a nationally known moderate Republican who opposed additional slave states.

The fateful year of 1860 saw the Democrat Party split into northern and southern factions, with each running a candidate for president. The Republican Party nominated Lincoln instead of William H. Seward, the radical from New York. Two months before the election, Nathan took his family to Cleveland to see the dedication of the Oliver Hazard Perry Monument.[39] Newspapers estimated that seventy-five thousand people came that Monday to the city: "Fathers, husbands, brothers, and sons; mothers, wives, sisters, and daughters went to bed at rest as to the character of the coming morn, and alarm clocks were set for an early start. At an early hour, wagons were seen entering the city by every avenue from the country. The early trains were crowded, each one adding its hundreds to the numbers in town."[40]

The normally dusty streets of Cleveland had been wetted down by heavy rains a few days earlier, and "the intensely sultry and oppressive weather… had given way to cool autumn air." The parade started at noon, winding around the downtown area and ending at the Public Square. In addition to a number of bands, there were numerous military units, including the Cleveland Grays, the Cleveland Light Artillery, the Cleveland Light Dragoons, the Hibernian Guards and the Cleveland Light Guards. "The Guards were out in their new brilliant Zouave fatigues dress and were accompanied with Dodworth's Band." Along the route, the crowds cheered loudly. "There is a natural military enthusiasm in the human mind, and on such occasions, it will have vent."[41]

The ceremony began with a prayer given by the Chaplain of the Day, Reverend G.B. Perry from Natchez, Mississippi. Mayor George B. Senter accepted the Perry Statue on behalf of the city and then introduced George Bancroft, historian and former Navy Secretary. Bancroft started and ended his long oration with a reference to the coming crisis of 1860, although his topic was the hero of the Battle of Lake Erie, fought on September 10, 1813:

> *Fellow citizens of the United States! The defense of our country is not a burden to be shunned; but an inalienable right which we are to assert and a sacred duty which we are to fulfill. The love of the Union has wound its cords indissolubly 'round the whole American people. So then our last best word shall be for the Union.*[42]

* * *

Southerners were openly threatening secession if Lincoln became the next president. Rallies favoring and opposing the Union were held throughout the country. In the northern states, supporters of Lincoln joined groups called Wide Awakes. A farmer from Olmsted, Newell Nelson "went to Detroit to a political meeting, from 40 to 60 thousand and 3 to 4 thousand Wide Awakes present," backing the Union.[43] On the Saturday before the election in Cleveland, West Side Wide Awakes, including a detachment from Rockport, marched by torchlight to Republican Party headquarters in the city. Another demonstration ending at the Perry Monument was announced "by order of the Commandant" for Monday, combining "regiments" from both sides of the Cuyahoga River.[44]

On November 6, Nathan Hawkins along with most Ohio voters cast his ballot for Lincoln. A stanch Democrat, his father-in-law voted for Stephan Douglas, candidate for the northern faction of the party. Both Rockport and Olmsted gave Lincoln a majority, and throughout Cuyahoga County, the vote was almost two to one in his favor. A week later, Wide Awakes from Rockport

The Lincoln statue on Cleveland's Mall was a gift from local school children. Max Kalish completed his bronze sculpture in 1932. *Author's collection.*

and Olmsted joined others in a "Grand Jubilee" under the gaslights of Cleveland. "The principal streets will all be ablaze with tokens of rejoicing and of victory. Refreshments after their long march…will be provided for them at the Headquarters after the parade, thanks to the generous Republican ladies of Cleveland."[45]

On the very day of this celebration, the South Carolina legislature voted unanimously for a state convention to consider secession. Without opposition, on December 20, delegates passed an ordinance dissolving its union with the United States. Ten other states seceded by February 1, 1861, to form the Confederate States of America. Opposing any federal government action against the Confederacy, four states in the upper south remained in the Union, waiting to see what action Lincoln might take after his inauguration. Buchanan, the lame-duck president, did nothing except to declare secession unconstitutional. Newell Nelson, however, remained optimistic and "didn't mind [since] Old Buchanan is fast for the union."[46]

On February 15, 1861, the roads were muddy trails in spite of the mild weather. Nelson rode into Cleveland to see Lincoln and with the "going very bad, saw Lincoln and family [with a] good reception."[47] On his way to Washington, Lincoln stayed overnight in the Weddell House Hotel. Before retiring, he stood on the hotel balcony and spoke to the crowd:

> *Your large numbers testify that you are in earnest about something. Do I desire that you should think this extreme earnestness is about me? I should be exceedingly sorry to see such devotion, if that were the case. But I know it is paid to something worth more than any one man, or any thousand, or ten thousand men—a devotion to the Constitution; to the Union and the Laws; to the perpetual liberty of the people of this*

country. There is one feature that gives me great pleasure; and that is to learn that this reception is given, not alone by those with whom I chance to agree, politically, but by all parties. If Judge Douglas had been elected President of the United States, and had this evening been passing through your city, the Republicans ought, in the same manner, to have come out to receive him. If we don't make common cause and save the good old ship, nobody will pilot hereafter.[48]

* * *

Joseph Root of Olmsted volunteered for the 23rd Ohio Infantry. Two future presidents, Rutherford B. Hayes and William S. McKinley, served in the regiment. *Olmsted Historical Society.*

A month after his inauguration, Lincoln sent provisions to Fort Sumter in the harbor of Charleston, South Carolina. Before the ships arrived, shore batteries fired on the Federal garrison, which surrendered two days later on April 14, 1861. Lincoln called into federal service seventy-five thousand militiamen for ninety days to put down the rebellion. Then, four more states left the Union. Caught up in the excitement of the times but too old to serve, Nelson "went to Camp Taylor [in Cleveland and] saw the soldiers and other warlike demonstrations."[49]

After the Confederate victory at the Battle of Bull Run in late July, Lincoln signed two bills authorizing 1 million enlistments for three years. Philip C. Hayes, a student at Oberlin College, wrote of the uncertainties of the future: "As time progressed, it served clearly to reveal to us the fact, which at first was not so patent, that the Rebels were both determined and united in their efforts to destroy the Union and establish an independent Government."[50]

Trying to do her part on the home front, Sabrina made pillows for the soldiers. When John Spencer joined the 15th Ohio Light Artillery in January 1862, she saw him off at his father's Rockport farm, where runaway slaves had been hidden over the years.[51] Six months later, Lincoln issued another proclamation for more three-year regiments. Charles and Francis Frost, Sabrina's nephews, decided to enlist in Battery E of the 1st Ohio Light Artillery, which had already seen action in Kentucky.[52]

In the meantime, Nathan Hawkins still lived the comfortable life of a civilian while Lucy's cousins endured the hardships of soldiering. However, he had a family to support in addition to having concerns about his father's well-being. Although elderly, Russell Hawkins served as chorister for the Congregational Church.[53] Perhaps Nathan did not share the religious zeal of his father, since he was not always at church on the Sabbath. Instead, he stayed home with the *Herald* and read "the war news and everything else that was readable [and] used to finish reading about the time Sunday school was out." Later in the day, he enjoyed having one of "those little girls on my knee or sit and talk with some neighbor that may have happened to step in. Then I can say a happy time has come."[54]

* * *

In June 1862, Nathan may have felt even more reluctant to volunteer after Lucy gave birth to another daughter, Nettie. All along, he assumed his brother James would "enlist but he did not talk as if he should do so. [Then] I thought it my duty that one of us should…in defense of our country." Obviously, the speech of George Bancroft had not been forgotten. However, Nathan was not an abolitionist like his father, and "as for my fighting to free them and have the slave stand and look on, I do not believe in it."[55]

Lincoln's call for 300,000 more volunteers on July 2, 1862, led to further debate over his war policies. There had been victories in the West, but the Federal army continued to suffer defeats in the East. Later in the month, the *Morning Leader* published an address by congressional Republicans declaring, "the Republic has the right to live—the Republic has the right, therefore, to enact all laws…to suppress an insurrection." On the same page, the *Ashland Union* denied, stating, "[It] is a damned Abolitionist war, [and] Abe Lincoln is as big a traitor as Jeff Davis."[56] Under the article, a new advertisement appeared in the newspaper:

> *Rally to the Rescue. EXCELSIOR COMPANY, 103d REGIMENT, commanded by Captain M.L.M. Peixotto...Men of Cuyahoga, Medina & Lorain! In this hour of our Country's peril, you are called upon to rally to... the preservation of the Union...$100 Bounty. $25 paid in advance. $13 first month's pay in advance. $50 by the City of Cleveland. $2 for every man enlisted. NINETY DOLLARS IN ALL before you leave Camp Cleveland!*[57]

Now a captain recruiting for F Company of the 103rd Infantry, Philip C. Hayes knew that the "first glow of patriotic fire had died away, and the second sober thought had succeeded." Many had second thoughts because the "death of many of our friends and neighbors had taught us that war meant danger." Federal soldiers had suffered more defeats than victories, and foreign intervention was a looming possibility. Even supporters of Lincoln began to "doubt whether it was possible to conquer the rebellion."[58]

During the evening of August 12, "a war meeting" took place in a crowded Rockport church. Captain Moses Peixotto recruited "some of the best material in the village as members of his company. His manly and soldier-like bearing and words made a most favorable impression, and a still larger number of recruits are expected from the township."[59] Nathan Hawkins, Frank Campbell and Orson Jordan were among those who enlisted that Tuesday night. Considering family responsibilities, Nathan's decision to enlist seemed at first to be illogical, since two-thirds of Union volunteers were unmarried. He had just celebrated his thirtieth birthday, making him four years older than the average enlistee. At the same time, he could be drafted if local quotas were not filled by volunteers. However, draftees did not receive bounty money and were seen as unpatriotic by their neighbors.

At another meeting in West Rockport, Captain Peixotto had problems getting enlistments until an attractive young woman addressed the quiet crowd. According to the *Daily Herald*, the woman said her brother had just volunteered for G Company. "Who would be the first to sign his name after his?" Amongst the cheering, five men came forward and volunteered.[60]

Over the next week, five more Rockport men enlisted into G Company: Robert Fleury, Ansel Jordan, Willie Lewis, Thomas Farmer and Warren Coe. Others who joined the same company included Charles Knapp of Olmsted and Amasa Witham from Dover. Farmer was the oldest, at forty-four years of age. Another Rockport resident, John Andrews became a member of E Company. Davis Webster, the antislavery farmer from Olmsted, volunteered for C Company. Willie Romp, Lucy Hawkins's nineteen-year-old brother, had signed up for B Company three days earlier.[61]

Camp Cleveland occupied thirty-five acres of land in today's Tremont neighborhood. On the left, Cleveland Institute overlooks the camp below University Heights. *Courtesy of Chris Whipple.*

Recruiting for the regiment went well in the month of August, with nearly 100 men enlisting from the townships of Rockport, Olmsted and Dover. A total of 651 enlistees came from Cuyahoga County. Civilians played an important role by raising money for bounties. The *Morning Leader* declared, "Good for Rockport. In the town of Rockport, three persons obtained $3,000 in one day for the purpose of encouraging enlistments. That is the right kind of talk."[62]

On August 20, Sabrina and Henry Beach went to the Hawkins farm and said goodbye to Nathan "before he left for war."[63] He reported a few days later to Camp Cleveland. Another volunteer for the 103rd Infantry, Sam Ames of Olmsted described the site as a "large and beautiful plateau on University Heights," the name coming from an academy that had opened in 1850.[64] Barracks of rough-cut lumber, each holding a third of a company, had been hastily built, and recruits drilled without weapons on the parade ground. The 103rd Infantry had a crash course in military formations but no training in loading and firing a rifle. Old Prussian muskets were available only for guard duty.[65]

During his first days in the army, Nathan had to adapt to a soldier's life. He no longer had the freedom to come and go as he pleased. As a farmer, Nathan had been his own boss, but now he had to follow orders and a prescribed routine.

Hiram Van Guilder of the 103rd Infantry died in the prison at Andersonville, Georgia. His name appears on this monument in Eaton Township Cemetery. *Author's collection.*

The day began at 6:00 a.m. with reveille followed by roll call, breakfast, policing quarters, changing of the guard, sick call and company drill. Lunch at noon was followed by officer's call for recitation, company drill, recall, dress parade, roll call and supper at 5:00 p.m. Unless on guard duty, he enjoyed leisure time until final roll call at 8:30 p.m. and then "Taps," which meant bedtime.[66]

After supper, some recruits—with or without permission—left camp for an evening in Cleveland. Those without passes had to sneak back past the guards to make roll call. If caught, they spent the night in the guardhouse awaiting punishment in the morning. Saloons and bordellos were popular attractions. Drunkenness led to a disturbance in late August that resulted in the camp commander's appeal to stop beer and liquor sales to soldiers. Most saloonkeepers acted accordingly.[67]

Furloughs were issued in limited numbers. A member of Captain William Wilson's Company of the 103rd Infantry, Ames received a four-day leave to see his wife, Amelia, and their infant daughter. They lived on Butternut Ridge in Olmsted with his parents, John and Lydia Ames.

> *Headquarters Co. 103 Regt. OVI*
> *Brooklyn* [Township], *August 14, 1862*
> *Private Samuel H. Ames has furlough within the state of Ohio until the 18th day of August, at which time he will report himself at these headquarters or be proceeded against as a deserter.*[68]

Governor David Tod reviewed the regiment on August 23. Other units at the camp included the 105th Infantry and the 19th (Shields's) Battery. To feed the recruits, the quartermaster "laid in a heavy stock of rations…consisting of hominy, rice, sugar, coffee, potatoes and bread." However, blankets had yet to arrive from the government, and civilians were asked to donate any "clear quilt, blanket or comforter" for the many "suffering" soldiers.[69]

* * *

With only a week left at Camp Cleveland, Colonel James Casement, commander of the 103rd Infantry, allowed picnics for the ten companies of his regiment. "A stream of wagons bearing the fair daughters—the noble wives, mothers and sisters of the brave boys of Rockport" came into camp with a "profusion of good things" for the men of G Company. Captain Peixotto, "in response to loud calls, made a neat little speech, thanking the ladies for their kindness and consideration for his brave lads."[70]

The company picnics had been combined into one large goodbye party. In the middle of the parade ground, tables were placed in a square and then "loaded with good things—turkeys, chickens, roast beef, cold tongue, ham, biscuit and butter, pickles, jellies, pies…." After the soldiers stuffed themselves, they removed the tables, and "dancing, to the inspiring music of the two brass bands present, was commenced and kept up for two to three hours." An hour before sunset, the men marched in formation, and they "will ever remember the day with pleasure."[71]

A few days before the camp party, an article had appeared in the *Morning Leader*:

> *With this week closes volunteering and the consequent withdrawal of bounties. On the 4th of September, the draft surely comes, taking at the outside every third man, who must serve a period of nine months at $11 per month. The time is short for consideration, and those who would leave behind them a handsome sum for the support of those for whom they have to care.*[72]

On September 3, the soldiers of the 103rd Infantry received their bounties before departing at 6:00 a.m. for the Union Depot in Cleveland. Shields's Battery fired a captured Rebel cannon, and Clark's Forest City Band marched out of camp with the regiment. "Superior Street was filled with a dense crowd of curious lookers-on and friends of the boys. [It was] the wildest scene we have witnessed since the departure of our first volunteers—the Cleveland Grays."[73] "A very large number of people, mostly relatives and friends of the departing soldiers were at the depot to say farewell, and there were many tearful partings."[74] About 8:00 a.m., the regiment boarded two trains for the trip to Camp Denison in Cincinnati.

The following day, the first news of the regiment appeared in the evening newspaper: "We learn from this morning's *Columbus Senate Journal* that the 103rd passed through that city last night and received its arms at the depot. Now, all that is required is a few weeks' drill and our Cuyahoga Regiment will 'hold its own' against any field."[75]

Sam Ames did not leave with the 103rd Infantry because Wilson's Company had been reassigned as A Company in the 124th Infantry. He did not see Nathan Hawkins again until the following January, when their regiments were camped outside of Frankfort, Kentucky. In the meantime, Ames worked in the camp hospital. Compared to what came later, he saw his

In Tremont on October 11, 2003, John G. Whipple, William C. Stark and Chris Whipple dedicated this Ohio Historical Society Marker for Camp Cleveland. *Author's collection.*

time at Camp Cleveland as "one continued picnic."[76] In early December, he wrote to Amelia: "I think the pigs [from the Ames farm] done very well for weight. We are all well at this time in our bunks. The boys all are full of fun. I can't tell how long we shall stay…but not long I dare say. Kiss the baby for me, and I will kiss you myself."[77]

On Christmas Day at Camp Cleveland, Ames most likely felt homesick, writing, "I wish you a Merry Christmas and all the rest of the folks…[and] will try and come out next week if I can." On New Year's Eve, the regiment received orders to leave Cleveland the next day. "One or two boys were at

Dover on furloughs. I was sent out to notify them and so spent a few last hours at home. But long before dawn on the morning of Jan. 1, 1863, I bade my wife and little girl, aged five months, a long farewell. My aged parents bade me God speed with tears."[78]

Chapter 2

NORTHERN KENTUCKY

The 103rd Ohio Infantry arrived in Cincinnati at noon on September 4, 1862, crossing the Ohio River in the evening and camping in Covington, Kentucky. The regiment was attached to the 2nd Brigade, 1st Division, Army of Kentucky. Two days later, rumors spread that the enemy approached a few miles outside the city. "We were ordered to draw, cook and pack three day's rations and hold ourselves in readiness to move to the front."[79] After sunset, they marched three miles, and near midnight, camped at Fort Mitchell. On September 8, the regiment officially mustered into Federal service.[80]

Nathan Hawkins wrote his first letter home to Rockport on September 11. They had been out skirmishing, and "for the first time I shot at a Rebel. There were two upon a brick house [and] one upon a chimney." Without considering Lucy's fears, he wrote about picket duty and nearly being shot by friendly fire. An enemy soldier had supposedly been sighted in the night, and an itchy-fingered recruit in another company of the regiment fired into the darkness. "It went into the ground about three feet from my head. Firing is going on all the time between the pickets" of both sides. He did not expect any major engagement but noted, "We have to be in our entrenchments night and day."[81]

The regiment returned to Fort Mitchell after capturing without a fight seven men from Morgan's Cavalry. Nathan was still getting used to carrying his rifle, ammunition and rations on twenty-mile marches in hot weather. "After we went to bed, the long roll was beat. The word given, load your pieces. After loading, we went to bed with our guns under head." Nothing happened that night, but the regiment remained on the alert. Five days later, Nathan came into camp after being on picket duty for forty-eight hours. He received twenty-five dollars, the last of his bounty money, and expressed it home to Lucy. "Why do you not write me?" he asked her in a letter. His thoughts were on the State Fair, his children and the farm: "Have you thrashed, got the corn up, the barn built?"[82]

Frank Campbell missed his family: "I think of my babies as often as I do of my meals." He was also concerned about the available water. "It is nothing but pond water, and when it begins to boil, there will a green scum rise on it. I believe if we don't get where there is better water, we will all be sick." Like Nathan, he expressed his bounty money home. "Our lieutenant says the money is there where we sent it." Frank hoped Lucy would visit Mag as often as she could. He wanted the two sisters to enjoy themselves "until we return home again. Nate says tell Tute that he says if he don't get a letter before long, he will write you one and just sput [*sic*] in it. Why the devil don't you write?"[83]

Lucy had written him, but mail delivery to the regiment took up to three weeks. Nathan finally received two of her letters on the same day in early October. She told him that Russell Hawkins might have drowned while traveling on a ship that sank off the coast of California.[84] "Why could he not have been spared to come home and see his father and brothers and our children?" Lucy had dreamt about Nathan, which "was rather singular for at that time I was on picket duty and did sleep under a straw stack and took a severe cold too." He had been sick for four days but was feeling better. The weather was very dry, and the regiment might have to move camp because of the water problem. Rumors were circulating that the South had proposed "terms of peace and that the Generals have met together to compromise the matter." Nathan had talked to a reporter from the *Cleveland Herald* about the antiwar Democrats who opposed being conscripted. "He says that they have commenced drafting in Cleveland and that they tried to resist but they called out the troops and quelled the riot."[85]

Nathan's squad was "a nice happy family. It is composed of R. Fleury, W. Coe, O. Jordan, A. Jordan, J. Gasner, Wm. Lewis" and Frank Campbell. They were camped in a region that was "very hilly, rough broken country… right on the Pike. It is a very nice road to Covington." Next to the regiment's bivouac, Nathan saw a dead soldier from a Michigan unit who had blown "his own brains out" while mishandling a pistol. Frank Campbell did not trust the farmers around them. "They are good to our faces, but when our back is turned—dam them! Negroes and Negro wenches here are plenty and black enough, too."[86]

Confederate memorial pays homage to the Battle of Perryville, fought on October 8, 1862. The Union's strategic victory prevented Kentucky from being captured by the Confederates. *Author's collection.*

During the second week of October, the regiment was placed in reserve status. Nathan sat in "a miserable" schoolhouse, describing it as "made of puncheon plank that is logs hewed out about four inches thick and chinked up with mud." Besides picket duty, he drilled four times each day. "First is squad, then company, then battalion, then dress parade." On one occasion, Colonel Casement did not like the drilling of one of his companies and yelled for Captain Peixotto with G Company. "We went out on the double quick and performed before the whole regiment." Then the Colonel shouted, "Now God Dam it, see if you can do it!" A few days later "on account of water," the regiment marched six miles toward Lexington with the companies of Peixotto and Hutchinson in skirmishers ahead of everybody else. "So you see we have come to the top of the heap, and all on account of our officers."[87]

Like Frank, Nathan did not trust Kentuckians. "I have been in different houses. They claim to be for the Union, all of them, but I have my doubts about it." He looked upon their slaves with amusement. "When I go to a house, they will peak around the corner of the house, show their worry and dodge back. Some have runaway and are in camp with us."[88] In the meantime, Corporal Amasa Witham of Dover had had enough of army life and disappeared into the night.[89]

* * *

On October 21, the regiment took the road to Frankfort. "There were some sore feet and tired men" after marching fourteen miles in one night. Scouts reported "a large force of Rebels" somewhere ahead of the regiment. Frank Campbell and Willie Lewis had been sick but were feeling better. And Willie Romp of B Company "is fat and healthy." Nathan was also "getting very fleshy, and my mustache and whiskers are getting quite long." He had dreamt about Nettie. "I was holding her in my lap, and she looked up and said 'papa' just as though she had not seen me for sometime and wondering where I come from."[90]

The 103rd Infantry finally arrived in Frankfort on October 30, and the men were "tired and lame." The regiment had been selected to guard the state capital because of its "soldierly bearing." Although Kentucky was a tobacco-growing state, "it is very dear here and good for nothing." Nathan wanted Lucy to send him "two pounds of Leymans fine cut." He was out of money, having "lent some," but hoped "to be mustered for pay today." Then he thought of his two older daughters. "Does Carrie and Libbie sleep upstairs now? Do they have a candle, and mama to go with them yet and the door left open, too?" Lucy had written about visiting family and friends in Olmsted. "I want you to go when you can and as much as you can." He saw no chance of a furlough during the coming winter, but "we are all in hopes to be at home by spring."[91]

On the first Sunday in November, Nathan went to a Presbyterian church in Frankfort. The minister "was a first rate preacher. They had good singing, too, with an organ. We were seated by a Negro and attracted considerable attention." The residents of the city "are not unlike the people in Ohio in appearance and fashion, although there are few young men here, most of which are in the Rebel army [and] a goodly number of ladies in mourning." He felt most of those in Frankfort were Confederate sympathizers, but "we are very well situated here and there is a prospect of our staying here all winter."[92]

G Company had camped on the same hill as "Daniel Boone's monument which is held so sacred by Kentuckians." Nathan was as impressed with it as he had been with Henry Clay's monument in Lexington. From his tent, he looked down at the Kentucky River, "the water which we drink and cook with." Union soldiers were in the process of building a railroad bridge across the river. He thought the countryside was "most beautiful" around Frankfort and would "like to live here if it was not for the Negroes which are plenty enough." A runaway slave was living with his company, but no more were allowed to enter the regiment's campsite.[93] "The people are generally very

Before the Battle of Perryville, Confederates had controlled Frankfort and gathered in the Capitol Building to swear in a governor loyal to the South. *Author's collection.*

kind and hospitable, Union people especially. It seems as if they cannot do enough for us." Nathan was impressed with their horses and cattle. "The men and women all ride on horse back. [I] hardly ever see one in a buggy." As far as the military success in Kentucky, "I cannot tell," assuming the people back home had a better idea from reading newspapers.[94]

* * *

During the afternoon of November 11, Nathan had been on a sixteen-mile force march to Lawrenceburg, which looked "like Irish Town in Cleveland." G Company was temporarily detached from the rest of the regiment because of reports that enemy cavalry might be in the area. "The people of this village and county are mostly secesh, and they have no delicacy in saying what they think either."[95] In the town square, a monument stood "to those who fell in the battle of Buena Vista in Mexico with their names inscribed thereon. It's about ten feet high with an iron fence around it."[96]

G Company was not at full strength. "Warren Coe was quite sick when we left him, and Jacob Gasner thinks he is going to have the ague. Ans [Jordan] and Willie Lewis are in the hospital yet in Lexington." Rumors still circulated about the desertion of Amasa Witham. Charles Knapp heard that Mary Witham had received a letter from her husband. Amasa told her to meet him in Michigan because he was heading for Canada. The Withams did not own the Dover farm on which they lived and had little to lose by not returning. "I suppose you have not seen him," Nathan wrote Lucy. "If he is caught, he now will be shot."[97]

Nathan expressed his growing pessimism in a letter to his father. "As for the war, generally it is no nearer to an end than it was a year ago." His opinion had changed for a number of reasons since being in the army. "There are so many don't care kind of officers from Generals even down to corporals. There is a lack of energy." He thought the South would win the war "unless we have different managers." Then his thoughts were again on home and family. "Have you done the thrashing yet, and if so, how much grain did you get? How do those hogs look? I suppose you have them fattening by this time." He still hoped his brother Russell had survived. "It does not seem to me that he is drowned. I have faith that he may have been picked up yet.[98]

In the meantime, G Company had suffered its first death. "The Captain wants me to say that Dave Dailey is dead and wants you [Lucy] to let Hezekiah Daily know about it." Captain Peixotto sent a letter to the father, who lived in Eaton Township, but "thought in case he did not get it you could let them know it. He died of typhoid fever." Others in the company continued to be in poor health. "Warren Coe is quite sick with the bilious fever, and Jake [Gasner] is sick with fever and ague" in Frankfort. Nathan was still wondering about the fate of Amasa Witham. He wanted to know if Lucy had seen Mary Witham "lately or had she gone away. I should hate to be in his boots."[99]

* * *

On a Saturday evening in the middle of November, Willie Romp saw the "company that Nate is in come back again" to Frankfort. Two soldiers from G Company were promptly arrested and punished for misconduct that had occurred before the march to Lawrenceburg. They were "not only drunk but abusive to their superior officers." One of them had to walk around with a flour barrel around his shoulders and arms. "The other had to carry a long stick on his shoulders with both hands tied to it." But Willie's mind was soon elsewhere. "I would like to be at home so that I could go into the buttery or down into the orchard" in the Rocky River Valley.[100]

Off duty on Sunday, Nathan went to see Warren Coe in a Frankfort hospital. "There are so many of our family sick." Although still very ill, Jacob Gasner was "not in the hospital, for there is not room now." Nathan heard that John Andrews of E Company had passed away. "Did his father see him before he died?" He hoped the body would be brought home and buried in Rockport Cemetery. "Lucy, it must be hard for one to die so far away from friends and family." Ansel Jordan and Willie Lewis "are in Lexington yet. I do not know how they are." Frank Campbell was well again and "eats like a horse."[101]

In Kentucky on November 7, 1862, John Andrews died from disease at the age of twenty. He is buried in Fairview Park's Rockport Pioneer Cemetery. *Author's collection.*

Most of G Company was "tired and foot sore. You need not think that I was tired for I was not. As the boys say, old Nate is tough." Thomas Farmer and he had often "taken a tired comrade's musket and carried it for him when on a long march." While on the road, they were the only ones in the company who had not ridden "on a horse or in a wagon since in Kentucky. I guess I have bragged enough for once."[102]

Nathan heard rumors that the 103rd Infantry might be heading to Tennessee. He believed the gossip because the regiment had been issued "Enfield rifles and capable of throwing a ball one mile. They are very nice pieces much better than the previous ones, the Austrian rifle." He wanted to remain in Frankfort "for this is a good place to stay. The people want we should stay. We have had a great many compliments on our marches for our good behavior." Apparently, Colonel Casement had been given three days to decide whether to move his regiment to Tennessee or spend the winter in Frankfort.

With every letter from home, Nathan hoped to get a picture of Nettie. When would her "likeness" be taken? "I bought a Mexican dollar to send her." The problem was how to mail the gold coin safely to Rockport. "I want she should have it when she cuts teeth." He did not think his daughter would like "Uncle Sam's crackers. The boys call them Cincinnati platforms or a plank in the platform."[103]

The following week, Nathan again went to the hospital and took care of the sick for most of the night. "I am afraid Warren will never be any better. He looks very bad, but Jacob seems better I think." After the misery of the hospital, Nathan was "much provoked" by the Soldiers' Aid Society for charging the soldiers for mittens. "They think they are hard up. What do they think of us?" Union soldiers in Kentucky "do not have as good a place to sleep as their horses." The society members should go "to Hell where they belong." He would never ask these people for even "a pins worth again."[104] He was also bitter about officers' wives who had joined their husbands in Frankfort. "I wish mine was here and was able to support her at the hotel of this city, but I cannot so I will go on my way whistling."[105]

A few days later, Nettie's photograph arrived in a box filled with food sent by the families of different soldiers. Nathan thought she looked like Carrie as a baby except for her eyes. "But alas there was one thing wanting…Warren Coe is dead. He died about the time we were opening the box in the evening. He did not live to taste those nice things that his wife sent him—grapes and butter and cake." Coe was the fourth to die in G Company. "Myself and Mr. Fleury went and laid him out. We performed the rites of burial according to military rule." The coffin was placed in a cemetery vault, and the chaplain telegraphed north about shipping it home.[106]

Another funeral took place on Sunday. "We have to march to the music of muffled drums and tunes such as [the] Bonaparte March." Nathan told his wife that she should not be concerned about him because he was healthy but acknowledged that the future was uncertain. "I tell you Lucy, if I am sick, I shall send for you. It is want of care that so many die although there has but a few in this Regt. as yet." However, there was also good news. "Jake is getting better but is pretty sick yet."[107]

* * *

"It being Thanksgiving Day and having eaten a hearty dinner, I thought I would write you a few lines." Nathan liked the meal cooked by the ladies of Frankfort. "We had fresh pork, mutton, turkey, pumpkin and apple pie and biscuit, but there was hardly enough for so many hungry soldiers after living on Uncle Sam so long." The field officers drank too much whiskey "and made a disgraceful appearance after dinner." In the evening, he went out on picket duty, taking charge of six men.[108]

Nathan awoke the next morning "all covered with snow." Lieutenant Colonel James Sterling rode into "my post in full gallop and wanted to know who had command of these men. I told him that I had the honor, sir. Then he wanted to know where my men were. I told him that he could count them." After realizing his mistake, Sterling told him what had happened during the night:

> *One of our men got drunk on picket (He was not with me understand.) and left his post.* [He] *went to the State or Capital Hotel barroom with his rifle loaded and cleaned them all out and cocked his piece and threatened to shoot the Lieutenant Colonel. They took him and bucked and gagged him and brought him to camp in a wheelbarrow. The other man will have to be court marshaled that had the man under his charge.*[109]

On the first day of December, the prisoner was taken to Lexington for his trial. "His name is James Pomeroy, a [former] sailor. I think they will hardly shoot him but send him to work on the fortifications for three years without pay." Pomeroy felt remorse for his actions, but he had been in trouble in the past. Nathan believed him to be an awful soldier but "not so disagreeable as some others" in the company. Captain Peixotto, who was having health problems, went to Lexington in charge of the prisoner. "He came and bade me goodbye and said he was going home if he could. I told him he must see you." Nathan believed the captain to be "a good man" and thought Lucy would agree with him.[110]

The weather changed from snow to thunderstorms. Jacob Gasner continued to recover, and "Frank is getting almost as fat as myself." Nathan could "hardly get his pants together. I shall be as large as Uncle [John] Ames if I keep on." He worried about his father's poor health and wanted to be kept up to date on the situation. On the other hand, Nettie had her Mexican dollar. "Private Fleury says to tell Toot [Lucy] that we are all well and all he and Nate wants is our ducks to lay along side of us instead of these rifles."[111]

The 103rd Infantry had just been inspected by "Major General Wright [and] Major General Granger." Later in the day, Frank Campbell wrote to Lucy: "I want you to visit Mag as often as you can and pass the time off as happy as possible, for I know you are both lonesome. I know you and she must have your hands full more so than we do in camp." Frank had recently gotten a letter from his father, who feared he would not return home until after the next election for president. "I sincerely hope that will not be the case, and don't you the same."[112]

Three days later, on a Friday evening, Nathan sat on his knapsack to write a letter by candlelight while "the rest of the boys are talking and laughing." He had good news for Lucy. "You wanted to know who took Amasa W[ithams's] place. I have the honor of holding the position [of corporal that] he held, and I shall not disgrace it as he did." The battalion had been drilling most of the day. On dress parade, he was surprised to hear of Pomeroy's light punishment—"four months pay taken from him and two months close confinement and the last ten days on bread and water." Nathan had received a letter the previous night from Mr. Silverthorn. He had visited "my house and that things were the same as usual only Nate was not there." Nathan wanted Lucy to send more butter. Army crackers were dry and only tasted good with butter. The company was leaving Frankfort tomorrow "on a long scout. When we come back, I cannot say."[113]

G Company marched back to Lawrenceburg, and the weather turned frigid over the weekend. "The water froze in our canteens in our tents, and we have a stove, too...but we are well clothed and do not suffer." They had been cold when first pitching tents on unthawed ground. "Tonight we have plenty of straw, and the ground has got warm and...we shall sleep warm tonight." It being December 7, 1862, he surprisingly failed to mention their ninth wedding anniversary. Nathan had something else on his mind—a letter from Mr. Kinney back in Rockport. "I was not in a mood to receive such a letter tonight," he wrote. Kinney had said that Lucy wanted Nathan to get from his father "a deed of the land that the house stands on." Nathan wanted to know whether "father had said something or had been drinking and perhaps had found fault with you." Lucy should have let him know if she suspected that his father had changed the will. Mrs. Kinney should remind him "what I am fighting for, and you pay all the hired help and half the taxes also."[114]

Nathan put off writing his father until the following week. At first, he did not mention Lucy's concern. In spite of the cold weather, "your boy slept as sound as ever. I have so become accustom to hard fare that I do not mind it much." Then he wanted to hear his father's "opinion on the war question. Mine is that it will either be closed this winter or that we have to wait until another President is elected." He believed there would be foreign recognition of the South if the war lasted another two years. Finally, Nathan asked his father if he remembered the conversation about the "deed of a piece of land where my house stands? The reason why I speak about it now is that I may feel sure that my family will have a little home provided that I should never come back." He hoped his father would not take offense to this request, "but I feel life is uncertain and should like to know that my family has a shelter of their own."[115]

The next night, G Company was back in Frankfort, and Nathan found Lucy's letter waiting for him. "While the boys were pitching tents, I went to Willy's tent and read it." He wrote a letter back the next day asking for a Christmas box of butter, bread, apples, pepper, sausage, honey and mince pie. "One of our family had a box last night. His name is Adam Miller. He had some butter, a shirt, tobacco, two quarts of brandy and one of whiskey, one can of peaches, and one of quince. His sister sent it. He lives in Cleveland. He is a good boy." Nathan wanted Lucy to tell his father "to write a few lines to his boy some of these cold days."[116]

A week later, Nathan opened a letter from his wife and "was glad to hear that you…felt so well about matters at home." He was able to write to her because Fleury and Miller had given him paper and postage stamps. Lucy assumed he had "plenty of time to write. I have more to do than you think. I have to drill men and be drilled." Captain Peixotto had resigned, and Henry Pickands now commanded G Company. Nathan felt he was "just as good and full of fun" as Peixotto. Nathan obviously had no prejudice toward Peixotto, who was Jewish. "I told him to take a ride out to our house" in Rockport. After hearing about the Union disaster at Fredericksburg, Virginia, Nathan thought the course of the war was "rather dark at present. I am afraid we shall not be home by spring, as [General Ambrose] Burnside has retreated across the river."[117]

* * *

Four days before Christmas, Nathan yearned to be home for the holidays. "I wish that the three of us could be there with you. If we could pop in just as you were sitting down to dinner." According to rumors around the regiment, furloughs might be granted if one had important business back home. Nathan thought it would cost him two months wages "to procure a citizen dress and pay my whole fare besides." Food rations were now more abundant, and they had plenty to eat. Colonel Casement returned to the regiment after an absence of three weeks. "We fired three rounds and had quite a little time." Jacob Gasner was finally out of the hospital. "The boys are all well and feel first rate." Getting out of their tents in the morning, they would yell, "All quiet on the Kentucky River."[118]

After four months, the routine of the army had become commonplace for Private Hawkins, but he continued to write about his civilian life. *Olmsted Historical Society.*

By Christmas, Nathan was gloomy and depressed. "I feel lonesome tonight, in fact almost homesick." He wanted to know what his daughters got "in their stockings and did they enjoy their Christmas?" Rain fell all day, and they had nothing to do but sit in their tents "while you people in Ohio were enjoying your nice dinner with friends." The others around him shared his mood: "Fleury lies here in his blanket sick with the rheumatism and can hardly get up. Jacob lies by his side and they are both asleep. Frank lies or partly lies down leaning on his hand with his elbow on the ground and so it goes every night. But we all felt pretty sober for a day or two."[119]

His letter to Lucy was suddenly interrupted. "There goes the drum for reveille and the orderly sergeant says fall in for roll call…so good night." The next morning, the course of the war was again on his mind. He believed "much trouble exists in the capital at Washington. I hope they will all resign, President and all, and then there will be some prospect of peace." How peace would be made with the South he did not know. President Lincoln had "called for six hundred thousand more troops, but [I] hope he can't get them." If the war could not be won with the Union troops already in the field, then it was a lost cause. He feared "the government is making preparations for a war with England, but [I] hope not."[120]

In the meantime, John Hunt Morgan's Confederate cavalry had moved into Kentucky and on December 27 captured the Union garrison in Elizabethtown about sixty miles from Frankfort. His goal was to disrupt supply lines to General Rosecrans's army, which was about to fight a major battle at Murfreesboro, Tennessee. On New Year's Day 1863, the same day

Morgan returned to Tennessee, Nathan was in Louisville. "We have had a pretty hard time…chasing Morgan out of Kentucky. [I have] not slept 10 hours since last Sunday night."[121]

On December 28, the 103rd Infantry had been ordered to leave Frankfort. "We at once began packing, and about midnight, took the [railroad] cars for Louisville."[122] Nathan was surprised that they did not have to go on foot. Twice they left the city on a train going south about twenty miles to Shepherdsville, halfway to Elizabethtown. The regiment was "drawn up in line of battle more than a dozen times and always in the night. Twelve miles [to the south]…the battle was fought," and Nathan saw the wounded and felt "quite anxious to go and help the poor fellows. We could hear the cannon roar quite plain." Morgan had taken "800 prisoners before the battle commenced," and they were paroled, arriving at Shepherdsville "just as we did." They had surrendered without "firing a gun, but when they told us so the Col. said they could not take us without somebody [Confederates] getting hurt." Nathan believed Colonel Casement would never "be caught napping. I do like him and the major, but the rest I have nothing to say." He had been sure the regiment was going to see combat action. "I felt just as cool as I ever did, quite different from what I expected." [123]

"On the 3rd of January, 1863, we again took the [railroad] cars and returned to Frankfort. It was rainy [*sic*] quite profusely when we arrived. The next day dawned cheerless and cold; yet it was a day of universal rejoicing."[124] The enlisted men were being paid for the first time in three months. Nathan, however, was tired and cynical after having "not slept more than twenty four hours in the last week." Believing the South would win the war, he criticized Lincoln's Emancipation Proclamation, writing, "…and I hope that Ohio will secede pretty soon. I have seen enough of this nigger question." Opening Robert Fleury's Christmas box, they enjoyed the "bread, butter, chicken, goose, fried cakes, cheese, mince pie and a can of preserves." The box also contained a photograph of Fleury's wife—"his ducks likeness." Nathan told Lucy, "I wish you would send me yours."[125]

* * *

Since returning to Frankfort, the army food had improved. "We have better grub than we have had…pork and potatoes and plenty of it." There were some familiar faces now in camp. Nathan talked to men of Shield's 19th Battery who he had not seen see since Camp Cleveland. The tall soldier from Olmsted was not among them. "William Spafford is sick at Richmond Key. What his disease

William Spafford was one of the largest men in the Union army, standing six feet, seven inches and weighing three hundred pounds. *Olmsted Historical Society*.

is I have not learned." Davis Webster of C Company had been discharged because of illness and hoped to recover at home. Nathan had not received his Christmas box because the colonel did not want express packages sent to the regiment until returning from Louisville. "You had better go to the office," he wrote Lucy, "and see if it has been sent back."[126]

A few days later, a snowstorm hit northern Kentucky, and the railroads were closed down. "We have had no mail for four days, which accounts for my feeling lonesome." When the weather improved, Nathan told Lucy, "the snow melting so fast reminds me of time [and] how fast it passes away since leaving home." He had been in the army for five months, "the longest time that Nate was ever away from his father and family, home and friends." Insisting he was not homesick, Nathan thought of going back to Rockport and seeing "the folks for a couple of weeks and make some arrangements about the farm for another year." He would try to get a furlough if the regiment received more of its back pay.[127]

Nathan still did not think the war would soon end, "but as we have said before, we live in hopes." He expected to "see some hard fighting in spring and summer." The siege of Vicksburg, Mississippi, continued, and "the Rebels claim the victory at Murfreesboro…at least Southern papers say so." He wanted to see a battle "but do not want to be in one myself." Since being paid, a number of soldiers had deserted from the regiment. "There has been four from our company, and I wish four more would go…then we would have a better one." More would probably desert in the spring, "especially sailors, and they won't be no loss, for they don't make very good soldiers anyway." Nathan was proud to be in the 103rd Infantry, having heard in

Louisville that no regiment "appeared so much like gentleman soldiers as we did."[128]

As the snow and rain continued, the men built wooden floors for their tents. Nathan was comfortable and had time on his hands because it was too muddy to drill. They had "nothing to do but eat and sleep, write letters and talk, [but] we are tired of this way of living…sick of soldiering, of the war, of everything." Many soldiers from 104th Ohio Infantry "were fast becoming secessionists." He wanted to tell Lucy about the behavior of "our own officers that would astonish the natives" at home but could not at the present time. Lucy had visited Mrs. Fleury, who wrote her husband saying, "Nettie was the prettiest baby she had ever saw and looked just like Nate." He wanted to know if they were "sleigh riding like fury up north." The heavy snow in Kentucky was unusual, being "as much as I ever saw in Ohio at one time, but it has not lasted long."[129] The Christmas boxes from Rockport and Olmsted finally arrived but were nearly a month late:

> *Everything but the butter, cheese and cans* [candy] *were spoiled. Frank's shirts were alright, but the pies and cake bread and cookies and apples were rotten and moldy. We threw them all away. There were two parcels of cookies, and one of them was very good, but they tasted rather old and the butter tastes of the cheese a little but we can manage that very well. I thank you and all our friends interested in their contribution, for we feel just as thankful for the things as if they were alright.*[130]

Word had been circulating that G Company was "the worst company in the whole regiment for drinking whiskey." And the story back in Rockport alleged the soldiers received a whiskey ration. Nathan told Lucy there was no allowance and that anything the government might provide "would only be an aggravation. When Nate drinks, he wants enough to make him feel good or not at all." He had asked her for whiskey in the Christmas box "not because I hankered for it but for the novelty of it." She should not worry since "your boy has not drank a pint of whiskey since he left home."[131]

Gossip spread around the regiment and camp claiming they were going to get paid for two more months. "Also a rumor that we shall go to Vicksburg afterward. If we go down there, we may expect to see some fighting." But the regiments in the state's capital had helped to keep Kentucky in the Union. He thought Lincoln's Emancipation Proclamation had created even more Confederate sympathy in Kentucky. "As for this war ever being ended by fighting, it never will. So Nate wants them to settle it before long for he wants

Michael Houck volunteered for the 19th Ohio Light Artillery at Camp Cleveland. He lost his left eye in the war but remained with the battery. *Courtesy of Chris Whipple.*

to come home." He was bitter that the field officers had gotten furloughs but not the enlisted men, causing some to go absent without leave. Many deserters were now "being brought back in irons. If I were a single man, I would desert myself."[132]

Willie Romp in B Company appeared to be less discouraged than his brother-in-law. "We are all as well as usual though we have most all got bad coughs." He saw William Spafford, who had rejoined the 19th Light Artillery on January 27 after being released from a hospital in Lexington. "He is as fat as a hog." The foot and a half of snow had melted quickly, and the recently built railroad bridge was destroyed by a flooded Kentucky River. Each company sent a detail of eighteen soldiers to "make a road from the railroad to the city which is about half a mile. There was not hardly any mud there. It was only about knee deep. We had a gay time, but we only had to work that day…for we got back to camp long before night."[133]

On that same day, Nathan talked with Colonel Casement about the war. "His opinion is that we shall not be detained very long in the army." Unlike the colonel, he was not optimistic since they had heard the same story before. However, the regiment had "been very fortunate in escaping the battlefield and the dangers attending them." He thought again about not surviving the war and his daughters being without their father. "There are a great many temptations that call the attention of such young girls sooner than boys." Snow again began to fall but at first melted on the mud around his tent. He was getting "quite fleshy" and now weighed 176 pounds. Maybe after all "soldiering agrees with me." Since they had to mend their own clothes, he could now "handle my needle as well as the musket."[134]

* * *

A week earlier, Sam Ames had seen Nathan Hawkins for the first time in five months. "I have heard from the 19th Battery, and they are well. The 103rd regiment are going with us down the river."[135] As it turned out, the two regiments would go their separate ways and not see one another until the end of the year. The 124th Infantry marched to the outskirts of Elizabethtown. "We all went to rest in our tents with the ground bare or nearly so, and the next morning the whole camp was under three feet of snow, our tents crushed over us." The regiment trudged single file into town using a path made by horses. They were to be "quartered in churches. The Colonel went to all the saloons and drinking places, and securing the liquor, poured it out on the ground."[136]

The 124th Infantry left Elizabethtown at the end of January, taking the train to Louisville. They boarded the riverboat steamer *Diamond* bound for

Marching to Elizabethtown, the 124th Infantry passed within twenty miles of today's Lincoln Homestead Park. Lincoln's mother had lived in the house on the left. *Author's collection.*

Nashville. "During our journey down, the crew of the boat commenced a series of thefts among the soldiers, which was very annoying. Samuel Brown, who was a Wesleyan preacher at West View and North Olmsted, lost his wife's picture with a ten dollar bill in it. At length the officers put the whole crew under guard and commanded the boat themselves."[137]

The stay in Nashville was short, and the regiment marched on to Franklin, twenty-five miles to the south. Sam thought the countryside to be beautiful, but war was taking its toll. He picked a sample of cotton and sent it to his wife. "Our boys raided a Sesech smokehouse…and secured a lot of nice hams." The first deaths occurred in his company, all from disease. Loren Fitch of Olmsted received a box from home. "He came for me to go and eat supper with him. I went and ate the best supper I had tasted since leaving home. We had cake, bread and butter, apples and pickles, and it all tasted of home and Ohio."[138]

Around midnight on the last Friday of January, Nathan was sitting in the guard tent when he "heard a terrible cry of murder." Thinking there was more than one person yelling, "I ran out and over to the Colonel's tent." Casement appeared and asked who was screaming. "At the same time loading my rifle, I told him I did not know." Joined by others, they headed into the night toward the direction of the commotion. "The first thing Nate done was to fall down stepping in a mud hole and come very near breaking my neck and leg." He nearly knocked an officer down who held a revolver in each hand. "However, I jumped up, and away I went on the run for over half a mile, the cry still echoing." Finally, they came upon two runaway slaves, a servant and his wife, who had been working for the colonel of the 104th Infantry. After seeing the soldiers approaching, three bounty hunters disappeared into the darkness. "His wife done some hollering."[139]

On the same day, Nathan received a letter from Willie Lewis, who was still recuperating in a Lexington hospital. "He wants to get his discharge." But the army will "not discharge anyone until they were dead, and he says the doctors cut up bodies at a great rate." Lewis had worked on Benjamin Mastick's farm in Rockport before enlisting. In a letter to Nathan, "Mr. Mastick wanted to know whether Willie had those gloves" he had sent him.[140]

Sitting in the tent, Nathan looked up from his letter to Lucy. Robert Fleury, Frank Campbell, Orson Jordan and Thomas Farmer were also writing letters home. "Johny Nicholson and Alvin Rhodes have just come off guard and are eating their breakfast. Adam Miller is reading. Herman Rhodes…is whittling a stick. George Wagner is mending his stocking." Nathan finished his letter with "P.S. about that barrel of whiskey, it is the first I knew about it. I have never...done any such thing, and you can tell Sell Spencer and all the rest of the folks the same."[141]

Speculating on the war was always a major topic of conversation. The colonel and lieutenant colonel of the regiment had talked to Nathan and disagreed on when it would end. Casement "thinks that we shall be in Cleveland by the Fourth of July," and Sterling "can't see that the war is any near over than it was one year ago." Captain Pickands said Nathan would "be at home to harvest the wheat." His tent mates felt they would "not be in the service three years for if it cannot be settled ere that time it never will."

Inside the Cuyahoga County Soldiers' and Sailors' Monument, President Lincoln hands a rifle to an emancipated slave. Levi Scofield was the monument's architect and sculptor. *Author's collection.*

Nathan believed "if we get Vicksburg, it will cut off their main supplies for their army. It will have a great tendency to wind it up."[142]

Nathan was "not down on Old Abe so much as I am the Democratic generals. Those that are protracting the war. They do not care one fig for the country." Although critical of the Emancipation Proclamation, he was still a Republican. "As for my fighting to free them and have the slave stand and look on, I do not believe in it." In early February, however, he changed his mind. "I see by the papers that Congress has passed a bill authorizing the President to raise as many Negro regiments as he sees fit. Now that suits me. Let them fight for their freedom and…I am willing to help them."[143]

A few days later, Nathan stepped into the tent, took off his wet India-rubber poncho and sat on the floor. "It is raining very hard and just come in from picket with a headache," he wrote to Lucy. "I want a gold pen from Crittendens, some tobacco, two or three lbs. of fine cut from Lymans, and two pairs of socks." He also needed stamps because "I lent some, but when soldiers borrow they never pay back, and you know I never borrow." Nathan figured it would "take almost a wagon load of potatoes" from the Hawkins farm to pay for his requests, but he expected to be paid in the near future. "The boys are all well except Johny Nicholson. He was sent to the hospital" with typhoid fever. "How are all the folks at home?" At this time of the day, he guessed, "Libbie and Carrie are at school, Nettie asleep, Toot [Lucy] sewing…and mother, she is probably knitting." Nathan paused for a moment and watched Frank Campbell leave the tent "to draw fresh beef three days rations." Then he realized the pain in his head had gone away. "I know now what will cure the headache."[144]

Nathan received a letter from Lucy later in the week. She wanted his opinion of Lieutenant Colonel James Sterling because others in the regiment had written home complaining about him. Sometime before the army, Sterling's father had been murdered in Cleveland. "I remember well the piece he wrote after his father's death. He headed an asylum for inebriates, and I always think of it every time he has been drinking." Sterling was unpopular with the enlisted men because he was "very strict in a military sense." Having been a railroad contractor, he was accustomed to being "a boss over men which makes him so I suppose." But Nathan was usually treated well by him. "When I get lonesome, I take a stroll around camp and sometimes call on the Major or the Colonel. The latter is first rate company," but he could also be condescending.[145]

When Lucy's picture finally came in the mail, Nathan thought she looked "quite natural. I had rather had the old gal herself than the likeness, but your picture made me feel bad. You know how [?]" He had sent Lucy an army certificate allowing her to draw locally against his pay three dollars every other week. "As to my being a lieutenant…it was the first that I had heard from it since writing Mr. Hand and the rest of the folks. Supposed they had done nothing about it, had forgotten me entirely. However, it's a little satisfactory to know that a little notice has been taken of me." Except for Colonel Casement, Nathan was critical of the field and staff officers, but he usually got along with them. On one occasion, Captain Pickands said, "if a furlough was to be given to him or myself, I should have it in preference. I have the good graces of the officers if nothing else."[146]

* * *

On a night in late February, "we were ordered to load our rifles and sleep on them. Morgan is about making another raid in the state." According to sporadic reports, Morgan was around fifty miles from Frankfort. Soldiers of the 103rd Infantry had "three days rations in haversack knapsacks ready to start at a moments warning." In the morning, the regiment boarded a train and left their home away from home above the Kentucky River.[147]

On the way to Lexington, the conductor "wanted to put our captain's cook off the [railroad] cars. The superintendent of the railroad had issued an order not to carry any Negroes." The train stopped, but Captain Pickands refused to obey the order. Then he and Lieutenant Colonel Sterling had a heated conversation. Pickands said he would not obey "any order that the superintendent of a railroad issued." Sterling then told him to remove the man. With Pickands "looking at me and winking at the same time, I spoke just as you know I can." Corporal Hawkins told the Colonel "that nigger is not going off this car tonight without some fun…the boys all said, no." Pickands looked him in the eye and said, "Colonel, you can't get him off without a fuss." Sterling warned him, "I shall hold you responsible." Another member of the company spoke up: "You need not hold him responsible but just chalk it down to Company G."[148]

Colonel Casement had been sick and away from the regiment. "Everything goes wrong," Nathan complained, "when our Colonel is gone. The Lt. Colonel has the most enemies of any man I ever knew." Sterling did not really care if "the men suffer and more…he is mean in other things outside of military matters." Colonel Casement always knew "how men ought to be treated, and [I] shall be glad when he comes back."

During the first night in Lexington, G Company "slept in an engine house on a brick floor" and then pitched tents the next day on the bare ground as the rain fell. "It was pretty hard to leave our board floors and stoves." Before leaving Frankfort, they had eaten ham and canned peaches sent from Rockport but now "had nothing to eat but hard bread for four days." As far as the incident on the train, they had "the expectation of being arrested but have not heard anything of yet." In spite of sleeping on the wet earth, Nathan felt Lexington was "a much more pleasant place and the people much more agreeable."[149]

The regiment camped on the former plantation of the famous abolitionist Cassius Clay. "One of the most beautiful places I have seen." On the other hand, he was getting tired of "laying around doing nothing like so many hogs—eat, drink and lay down and grunt." Nathan went into Lexington to see Ansel Jordan and Willie Lewis at the hospital. "Ans looks first rate and Willie also. Ans cuts a big swell here with a watch and chain." Nathan wondered if they would be sent back to G Company. Lewis was now a cook in the hospital, and "the surgeon says Ans is the best nurse he has got."[150]

* * *

Instead of taking the train back to Frankfort, they fell into ranks on March 9 and began the twenty-eight-mile walk in the rain. "The roads were very muddy and sloppy. It was very hard traveling, and there were a good many lame boys." In the afternoon of the following day, the regiment marched into its old camp. Captain Pickands "was about used up," and Orson Jordan's "feet were badly blistered." Nathan had a blister on his heel "as large as a ten cent piece, and it's very sore." But it was good to be back in a tent with a floor. "Tom Farmer sits here picking over beans. Hope we shall have something to eat once more." Nathan did not like rice. However, they were "almost starved this noon but did not have anything but rice and sugar" for their lunch. Hungry and distraught, he was "glad they are going to draft again on Eli and George Kennedy's account. Hope they have to go."[151] The Kennedy brothers lived on a ridge named after the family in northern Olmsted Township.

Nathan had received a letter from his brother Eli , who lived with his large family in Mount Pleasant, Iowa. One of his daughters was "affected with paralysis [a lame foot] and about the same as your Libbie. I am glad that you went into the service so that our family may have one representation there. I think that father and your wife with a hired man will get along well enough." His twenty-year-old son Jones "was very anxious to go to the army but I thought him too young to stand it." Eli had lost a considerable sum of money in the grocery business. "Times have been getting worse every year since I have been here. Jones will help me some I suppose if he is fortunate on the railroad."

Nathan heard what he had long feared. Eli had read of their brother's death in a California newspaper. "I do not recollect whether Russell could swim or not. If he could and got near the shore, he probably could not get over the breakers. At any rate, he probably perished in less than three miles of the shore." Eli assumed Nathan wanted to know about his views on the war:

> *I think as you do that it has been badly managed. Still the government has accomplished a great deal and will probably accomplish a great deal more before grass grows again. One thing in my opinion is certain, and that is we shall never have any peace again until slavery is abolished. I hope your health will continue good until the end and that you may not be ordered further south.*[152]

The 103rd Infantry spent the week "digging trenches around these hills" in order to fortify the town with siege guns. "We all think that we shall see some very hard fighting in Kentucky this summer." By the following Sunday, Nathan was on light duty because of a severe cold. He had "some fever last night, but [I] feel a good deal better this morning. I took cold when we were marching from Lexington." Frank Campbell had a flare-up of rheumatism, but it was "not very bad." Ansel Jordan and Willie Lewis were back with the regiment. Lewis was angry because he had lost over thirty dollars. He thought someone might have picked his pocket.

The enlisted men were now being issued meat, which "was so fat and tasted so strong we could not eat it." Nathan complained to the lieutenant colonel and the two regimental doctors. "I told them if they would say they could eat such meat as that I would eat it." They did not know what to say. "I was as insulting as I could be. I expected they would arrest me but have not been as yet."[153]

A week later, Nathan was almost over his cold. "I do not have to work unless I have a mind to, but I thought as I had not done any duty for some time…it would do me good to shovel a little dirt for a change." He did not tell Lucy that his neck had swelled alarmingly. She thought he "appeared more cheerful of late. In fact, I feel a great deal more encouraged with the [war] prospects than I have in some time." There were reports that the "Rebels are starved out." Yet he expected to see "some desperate fighting" in the near future. He knew there were mobs in the North resisting the draft. Colonel Casement had been home on sick leave and heard someone "uttering treasonable sentiments in Painesville." He swore at the man and told him to get a gun because "I will shoot you" the next time I see you.[154]

Other thoughts of home concerned the money Nathan and Lucy owed her mother. Complicating matters were the politics of his father-in-law. "I suppose Mr. Romp holds to the same opinion that he held when I was at home," he wrote Anna Romp. "But it will do him no good. This government is determined upon this matter and will put this rebellion down." Except for having a family to support, he would like the army more, but "after all the hardships of a soldier's life, I can't say that I dislike it." Anna would be happy to know that "Willie is one of the provost guards of the city which is an easy berth for a soldier. Well Mother, I have never said anything about the money I owe you for the sheep." He wanted to go home and "see to these things a little this spring. But a furlough is out of the question." Nathan did not know when all the debt could be paid, but "Lucy can pay you once in a while as you want it."[155]

* * *

Nathan had grown tired of the rainy nights. Each day, he saw Kentuckians, white and black, plowing the wet soil. The fortifications around Frankfort were nearly finished, and the men now enjoyed a healthier diet. "We have had very good meat since the fuss. What meat the quartermaster had on hand at the time was condemned by the doctor." Lucy had worried about Nathan getting into trouble for complaining. "You need not be afraid of me being arrested for finding fault with the rations, for I know when meat is sweet and when it's not." Again there were concerns about the enemy. "They are in force about 35 miles from this place. Some of the 104th Regiment were taken prisoner and were here this morning with a parole [from the Confederates] on their way to Camp Chase" outside of Columbus, Ohio. "The Rebels said they were not going to stop until they saw the Ohio River."[156]

At the end of March, more rumors swept camp. "Burnside is coming with forty thousand of the Potomac army. The Rebels are all broke up into small guerrilla parties and are scouring the country." What Nathan knew for sure he saw for himself. A battle had taken place to the south. Federal troops took about two hundred prisoners, while the Rebels captured half that number. The Confederates reported as parolees to Colonel Casement. "The ones we took were brought in here yesterday and were started for Louisville this morning. They were a ragged greasy looking set, but they said they had enough to eat" from foraging.[157]

Nathan was again running out of tobacco and wanted Lucy to send him more. "Toot, do not think me greedy…I know its hard times and you have to work hard and put up with a good deal on account of my absence." As a corporal with responsibilities, he was already getting frustrated with Ansel Jordan and Willie Lewis. "Ans is sick again. He looks as healthy as I do, but he is bound not to do duty. He is too lazy I think." Jordan was liked by most of the soldiers in the company. "Willie is a pretty good boy, but he is very slack about keeping his things together. We have to scold him a good deal."[158]

On the second morning in April, Nathan's mind was more than ever on his home back in Rockport. "I have thought of those kittens a good many times. I expect the children have handled them so much that they lay in the chip pan all the time. But I suppose they are entitled to handle them some since they have become so smart as to get a meal of victuals." Nathan's army family now included Jerome Stockwell, Ansel Jordan, Johny Nicholson, Willie Lewis, Adam Miller, Frank Campbell, Orson Jordan, Thomas Farmer and Robert Fleury. Except for Nicholson, who was hospitalized, they were either out on work detail or gathered inside the tent. Two runaway slaves lived with G Company. One of them Nathan called "first rate, [and] he says when we go home, he is going to live with me."[159]

After finally being paid on Saturday night, the regiment took the road out of Frankfort the next morning and walked fourteen miles to Versailles. "We marched the next day nearly 20 miles to a town called Nicholasville," where Nathan wrote Lucy a hasty letter about moving south and expressing her forty dollars. It was not until Friday night that they reached their destination, a campsite near Stanford, Kentucky. "Here we are after a march of seventy five miles since Sunday. We passed through a good many towns and a very beautiful country." They had gone through a place where Federal troops had fought Rebel raiders. Cannonballs and grapeshot lined the road for a mile. "Some places the ground was covered as thick as apples under a tree." The weather had been good during the week. Around Stanford, "people are plowing and planting. The grass looks very green. Peach trees are in bloom." He wanted her to "write and tell me all about the farm. How are those little girls?"[160]

A reporter from the *Cincinnati Commercial* saw the regiment making camp and wrote an article that appeared two weeks later in a Cleveland paper. "The 103^{d} Ohio and 2^{d} East Tennessee are about to exchange their old-fashion" large tents for the two-man pup tents. The new shelter was better for a soldier on the road because he could carry it himself and not have to sleep without shelter. "All are soon as comfortably fixed as soldiers can be who are on the march."[161]

A few days later, Nathan wrote, "Today is the Sabbath. We have had company inspection as usual. Today is the 12th of April. Just eight months ago today, Frank and Orson and I enlisted. Time has passed very rapidly with me." Nathan and Frank had sent their winter clothes and blankets home. They were heading farther south and "had to lighten our knapsacks and such a pile of clothes that was thrown away you never saw." In addition to a knapsack and pup tent on their backs, they also had to carry "haversacks filled with three or five day rations, forty rounds of ammunition, a canteen full of water" and a heavy rifle. "I am not very anxious to get into a fight, although I should like to see a battle." Lucy had hoped his regiment never saw combat. "I cannot say as I do so wish, for when we come home we should be called the bloodless 103 [Regiment], and that would not set very well."[162]

The 2nd Ohio Cavalry camped nearby, and soldiers of G Company went to see old friends and relatives from back home. Afterward, they took down their pup tents "for the purpose of airing the ground. You have no idea how filthy a tent will get in one week." Nathan was angry with Willie Lewis, who shared the tent with him. "As I have charge of the tent, I have to jaw him all

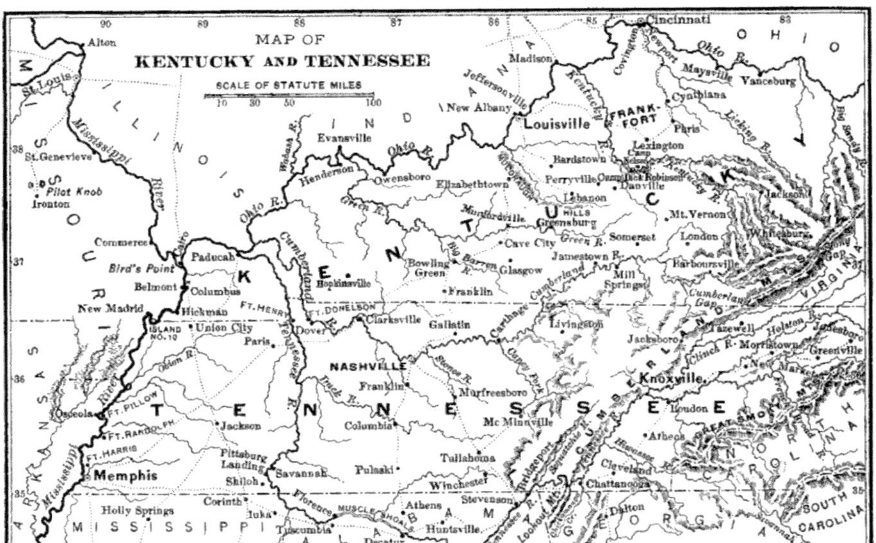

The Cumberland Mountains formed a natural barrier to any Union invasion of eastern Tennessee. An important railroad junction, Knoxville became a major objective for General Burnside. *The Century Illustrated Monthly Magazine*.

the time. He will finish dinner, perhaps leave his plate and cup laying around perhaps a chunk of meat and two or three hard breads [then] go off and play [base] ball. He was put on extra duty for not keeping his rifle clean. He is the worst or slackest soldier I ever saw."[163]

Nathan received encouraging news from back home. "The Union ticket was elected in Cleveland, also in Olmsted. Wonder how your father feels about [the election] this time. [I] am glad James Potter was elected director head" of the schools in Rockport. Lucy had been boarding a teacher who needed a job for the next term. Nathan wanted Lucy to see Potter, a Union man, about hiring the teacher. "You must try if you want to board the teacher," which brought in extra income for Lucy and provided "a good deal of company for" his wife. Aunt Sabrina Beach stopped for visits, but she was busy with her own family and seamstress business. "Give my respects to Sabrina in return."[164]

Chapter 3

Southern Kentucky

"Our quiet camp life at last drew to a close," wrote Captain Philip Hayes of F Company when the 103rd Infantry left Frankfort. "With the early days of spring, the enemy again took the field."[165] Frank Campbell thought "this hot sunshiny weather in April does make us northern lads feel rather lazy. But soldiering is the laziest life or job I ever got at yet." They were camped in Lincoln County, where "there was but one man that voted for him," an owner of a hotel in Stanford. "The Rebels are only across the Cumberland River," thirty-five miles from the regiment.[166]

Nathan had shown Frank a passage from one of Lucy's letters. She now knew "how to appreciate a husband or forgive all old difficulties if Nate was only" home again in Rockport. "No doubt you received my overcoat by this time," he wrote back to her. "I want you to wash it so it will be ready for me to wear next winter." She had sent him a pen that "is not gold. It looks as much like iron as anything." He had mailed her "a register of our company which I want you to frame for me that we may have it to look at in after years." Had she read "the puff the 103rd Infantry got in the Frankfort paper?"[167]

On April 21, 1863, the *Cleveland Morning Leader* published a "eulogistic article" from the *Frankfort Commonwealth*, a Unionist newspaper:

> *This splendid regiment, having received orders from headquarters to rejoin their brigade, left the city on Sunday morning for a more active field of labor. Our people regretted very much their departure. Having been on duty at this post for about five months, the citizens had the best opportunities of*

> *judging of the character of the men. In all respects, they behaved themselves in a manner to reflect credit upon themselves and honor upon the cause in which they were enlisted. Ohio may well feel proud of the 103rd Infantry. They will never dishonor their state.*[168]

Late April in Kentucky was "as warm as I ever saw in Ohio in June." The regiment was in "a very pleasant camp ground" with a good spring for drinking and cooking. Nathan was "wondering how it looks away up in Rockport…wish I was there to eat jonny cake." Lucy was given instructions on how many lambs to raise and sheep to sell. The grass in the new meadow would have to be abundant to "keep what stock you got, but if it don't, I think you had better sell some of those two year olds or a cow or two rather than buy hay every spring." Not wanting to worry her, Nathan confessed that until recently he had "not spoken a loud word for a month." He was almost recovered from the cold that had caused his neck to swell. "Except [for] us sick ducks," the regiment left camp on the following afternoon and took the road to Somerset, located five miles north of the Cumberland River.[169]

A day later, Willie Romp arrived with B Company in Somerset. "We remained about noon the next day, then we started for the Cumberland River." The regiment spent four days traveling along the northern bank of the river in search of enemy troops. On the fifth day, "we started for the river which we crossed about nine a.m. After our regiment landed on the other side, we went up the hill and went into the woods to wait for the other" five regiments of infantry and cavalry. On seeing the size of the Union army, the Rebels retreated under fire about fourteen miles. The skirmishing ended at dusk, and they made camp for the night.[170]

In the morning, the Federals "drove them from Monticello, where they had been encamped for about five weeks and lost one man—the Bugler of the 2nd Ohio Cavalry." A sniper in the courthouse had shot him dead. The 103rd Infantry camped in the town four days before marching back to the Cumberland River for the return to Somerset. Romp wrote:

> *Our regiment went over first, and they* [the 27th New Jersey Infantry] *was next to us and the boats would only hold about 50* [soldiers] *at one time. And they was in a hurry to get over…. About half the regiment had got over when one boat started out with about 60 men in it, and the current was so strong that it upset the boat and 32 of the poor fellows went down to rise no more. I think that was pretty hard, for their time would have been out this month.*[171]

Greg Adzema drills sharpshooter re-enactors during a Military Timeline event at Frostville in the Rocky River Reservation of the Cleveland Metroparks. *Author's collection.*

A week later, on May 12, Nathan rejoined his regiment and was well enough to be on duty in charge of twelve soldiers. "I am away from camp about three miles on picket in a dense forest. Will be relieved at 12 o'clock today. It is the most dangerous post of any. Have been up all night." He was ecstatic after hearing that Richmond, Virginia, had fallen to the Union army. "The war is virtually at an end," he wrote. After returning to camp, he heard the Confederate capital had not been captured and that "General Hooker has been whipped." Once more, the war seemed endless along with the time when he would again see his family. However, Orson Jordan was about to get a furlough if General Burnside signed the leave papers. Nathan had first choice, but "Orson's folks are dividing their property…and it will cost two or three months [pay] to go from here, and you know that we can't afford that."[172]

Nathan heard from Willie Romp that the regiment had been close to seeing action across the Cumberland River. "If the Rebels had not run, the boys would have made them," but other Federal troops had skirmished with them. "Our men found in an old barn 30 dead Rebels laid away thinking our

Thirty-six Civil War veterans are buried in Fairview Park's Rockport Pioneer Cemetery, including four who died from disease during the war. *Author's collection.*

men would not find them…but they did and dug a hole and dumped them in, good enough for them. But I do not want our men buried that way."[173]

His brother-in-law was sitting nearby also writing a letter. "You ought to see Willie," Nathan told Lucy. "You would hardly know him. He has grown some and thickened up a great deal. You know he used to be so bashful. He has got bravely over that and appears very manly." They had more time to visit, since drilling was only once a day "at six o'clock in the morning… when it is cool. It gets pretty warm down here now." The only other duty was picket, and sometimes, "the Lt. Colonel wants me to go and play a game of [base] ball."

During his leisure time, Nathan enjoyed walking around Somerset. One day, he went into a cemetery, where a marker on a woman's grave caught his attention:

> *The stone was a common river stone, worn and weather beaten by time. I sat down and with my knife scraped off the moss and found that the occupant was born in the year 1719. The date of death I could not make out. Time had worn it away. It reminded me of father's visit to Connecticut, hearing him tell about the graves of his old friends.*[174]

* * *

Near the end of May, the regiment moved to within a mile of the Cumberland River. Confederate soldiers had reoccupied the southern bank after the Federals had withdrawn back across the river because of supply problems. "I was down to the river last Monday, and as I approached the bank, I saw a Rebel cavalryman. He drew his saber and shook it at me. I drew my rifle to my eye, and had it not been for Captain Hutchinson, he would have been a dead Rebel." According to a truce, pickets were not supposed to fire on one another, but the next day, the respite ended. "Now we hear picket firing nearly all the time." Corporal Hawkins had charge of four privates on overnight guard duty, and they were "the farthest in advance of any [picket]. It seems to be my lot to have the most dangerous post of all, but it suits me well enough."[175]

The regiment had camped "in a beautiful grove at the base of the Cumberland Mountains. The crops look well. Corn is hoed once. Wheat is heading up. The meadows look extremely well." Nathan looked up from his letter and saw four slaves who "have toiled day after day working as though they were waiting only for time to pass away. No interest in anything. They have to be goaded along as we would an ox." He did not think them equal to white people. "They are far inferior, but they have as much right to be free as I have." Clouds were gathering above the mountains, and it looked like a storm was coming. There had not been any rain for a few weeks. Except for the slaves, everything seemed natural and peaceful:

> *Still time passes and seems to have no effect that is unusual on anything. People die, marry, and given in marriage, children born but what of that. It is all vanity…and if I am to die in the army, one thing is sure—I won't have to die but once.* [I] *am bound to see this rebellion put down and feel it is an honor to be an American soldier. And more than that even am proud to know I am a northern man…where all men are alike* [and] *have an equal chance for an education.*[176]

Nathan spent the rest of the afternoon washing clothes and cleaning his rifle. A dinner of salt pork, pea soup and bread was interrupted by "a dispatch that the Rebels were crossing the river at Town Points, Mill Springs and Fishing Creek. We had to fall in and stack arms while we were eating." His regiment was the only infantry along the river, as the others had gone back to Somerset with rumors of being sent to Vicksburg. "We are here to watch the Rebel movements. If they are too much for us, we shall have to fall back to Somerset."[177]

Five days later, the regiment was still camped in the same place, but orders came that Tuesday night "to dispose of all extra luggage and pack five days rations in our knapsacks besides put three days more in our haversacks and get ready to march." Frank Campbell believed they were heading across the mountains to Knoxville. Friday arrived, however, and the 103rd Infantry continued to wait for four companies doing guard duty in Somerset. Rumors about Vicksburg had been correct, and two brigades left town on the way to Mississippi. "I had rather not go down that way at present," Frank told Lucy, "for I think there will be some awful hard fighting there."[178]

Eight years earlier, Frank had married Mag Romp and promised to "stay with her through all the trials and temptations of life, to be one another." If Frank had kept the promise, he "would not be out in the woods writing letters." Feeling guilty and angry, he resented northern "aristocratic husbands" who could avoid fighting for their country. "I would like to have them on a march," cursing and complaining. Soldiers were often surrounded by temptations. Lucy had asked him about seeing "wickedness and sin. Well I do not know hardly what a Christian would call it. But I know it is a good place to learn if anyone is inclined that way."[179]

After their marriage in Olmsted on January 1, 1856, Frank and Mag Campbell went to Cleveland and posed for this tintype. *Olmsted Historical Society.*

Robert Fleury's wife had told Nathan in a letter about the high wages back home. Nathan hoped this would also mean higher prices paid for farm production. He told Lucy not to sell the wool too quickly. "You know we sold in too much of a hurry last year…suppose crops are not as far advanced as they are here." The Kentucky weather continued to be very warm during the day, but at night, it was quite cool. The night before last, they had been out supporting a cavalry raid on the southern side of the Cumberland River. At sunrise, "pop went some guns, and in a few moments, in come the 2nd Ohio Cavalry with five prisoners. So they kept it up all day. Two of the [cavalry] companies were surrounded and had to cut their way out. But they brought 42 Rebs with them."[180]

An obstinate and parsimonious man, William Romp did not support Lincoln's wartime policies. Neither Nathan Hawkins nor Frank Campbell liked their father-in-law. *Olmsted Historical Society*.

Nathan's spirits were again very high. "If I live to get out of this and the war is not over, I shall enlist again," he told his forlorn wife. "But I have not the least idea the war will last our term of enlistment." Peace Democrats, however, like Clement L. Vallandigham, were prolonging the war. Vallandigham had been nominated for Ohio governor even though Lincoln had deported him to the South after being convicted of sedition. Not welcomed by the Confederacy, Vallandigham was transported to Canada. "Your father must be crazy. I think he wants to know that Ohio soldiers have got something to say this election. They have a vote as well as him. I hardly think Mr. V. will hold another office very soon in Ohio. But we are hoping for the best and believe will come right in the end."[181]

After sending money home with a private going on furlough, Nathan enjoyed some leisure time until he heard orders "to put two days rations in haversack and march." The cavalry was again harassing the enemy on the other side of the Cumberland River but had run into Rebel reinforcements. "We crossed the river just at dark. We had to wade across and such a time you never saw. Some pulled off all their clothes, some only their pants, some not anything. Some fell down while the rest laughed…it was fun alive." Once across, the men marched a mile up a steep hill, where they made camp and slept under the stars. In the meantime, the cavalry "retreated under cover of night and arrived at the river about daylight." Nathan talked to Charley Nicholas, who "was in the fight. They had seven wounded, two mortally, one a lieutenant." After returning to camp, Nathan decided, regardless of the cost, that he had been away from home too long. He took part in a draw for a furlough but lost.[182]

* * *

Orson Jordan returned from Rockport and brought letters and newspapers as well as tobacco from Lucy. "The tobacco tastes very natural," Nathan told her. The antiwar sentiment in Ohio angered him. "When I read about those Copperhead conventions, those sympathies of treason that I should like to meet them on the field of battle. I would stop firing at the real enemy and turn my rifle upon them." An orderly from his regiment told Nathan that soldiers are "looked upon as some low contemptible thing" by these people. If he were to come home on furlough and be harassed "in any way or form, someone will get hurt, get their nose broke perhaps." He had not enlisted to be a "loafer or thief," as these people charged. "A person can retain his character and preserve their dignity as well in the army as at home [even though] there are a great many temptations."[183]

Something else had upset him. Orson Jordan said there was a rumor going around at home that had been started by Eastman Bradford of Olmsted. In late winter, Bradford went to Frankfort to see his son, who was sick with typhoid fever. Upon returning home, Bradford claimed to have seen Nathan "walking the streets of Frankfort city with a nigger wench." Nathan told Lucy that he had never been "walking with any female, white or black." Her husband was "just as virtuous as when at home." He had seen Bradford a number of times in Frankfort. "What a fool he must be to tell such a thing even if it was so. If I ever come home, I shall ask him about it. I care nothing about it only for your sake." Jordan and others spoke to Bradford and "gave him all he wanted."[184]

Besides wild rumors back home, Nathan also had concerns about his father. "It made me feel sad even to the shedding of tears," he wrote him, "when you spoke of your age and the cares you have." Yet he did not regret enlisting, since "some think they owe their duty to their country first, but it seems not so to me some times." Russell Hawkins wanted his opinion on the war. "To me, times look dark." Anti-war Ohioans "give no encouragement toward putting down this rebellion." They had nominated Vallandigham for governor, "a traitor to this government. One too that has been banished from his home." Then, the draft "coming on and the political excitement together makes men think and talk but what the result will be is yet to be seen."[185]

Two days later, on a Saturday morning, the regiment started on a forty-mile march to Monticello. They crossed the Cumberland River around noon and reached the town early on Sunday morning without suffering any casualties. "The Rebs had all left but a small force. Our cavalry drove them two miles beyond the Tennessee line." The natural scenery was pleasing to the eye, "but the farming interest looks very desolate [with] fences torn down…crops torn up" from the recent fighting. At one time, Monticello had been "a flourishing village, but cruel war has made it a desolate town." After a stay of only two days, they returned to their camp across the river. "As the boys say, we had a very dusty time coming back."[186]

Willie Romp in B Company felt "a little lame after our march." For the first time, he had not been able to keep up with the rest of the men. "I was not the only one that fell out, for there was about fifty or more." He spent the night with Charles Brown and Hiram Bradford in an oat field. "In the morning, we went on the rest of the way." The weather had been hot, but "since we came back, it has rained steady all day." Private Brown decided to celebrate the return to camp. "Our sutler [civilian merchant] keeps beer, and Charley went up there and got so drunk…[that] he went into the woods about two hours ago and threw up Jonah awhile and then laid down and slept." Waking up, Brown thought it was the next day until Romp told him differently.[187]

Like his brother-in-law, Nathan had struggled during the march but did not fall out. His exhaustion brought on more anger toward the antiwar dissenters back home. "I am ashamed of my state, of my country, my town and neighbors." Another draft was on the horizon, and protestors threatened to disrupt it. "I actually hope if they do resist that northern Ohio may see and feel the effects of an army passing through the country." Farmers would see their fences chopped up for firewood and livestock taken for food. If the weather is rainy, "they will dig little trenches all around their tents, thereby spoiling the meadows." He wanted Lucy to warn the people what could happen to Rockport, Dover and Olmsted. "If I were called home to quell any disturbance, I should neither spare friend or foe as regards their

Feeling nostalgic on his birthday, Nathan Hawkins may have thought of Lucy as the twenty-year-old Miss Romp, whom he had married in 1853. *Olmsted Historical Society.*

property. I think of the friend if he were at home that he ought to be in the battlefield. If they are Union people, they can afford to give it us."

Nathan sat barefoot looking at the mountains beyond the river beneath a rising moon. He wondered if Lucy was on their "porch looking at the pale empress of the night. Am sure if you were doing so you were thinking of Nate." Did she realize the date was June 23, 1863? "Nate is thirty-one years of age today." In his weariness, he had trouble recalling the date when Nettie was born. "Well do I remember the circumstances that attended her birth." She had also been born in June. "Times change and pass away." But Lucy must not think the army had changed him adversely. "I am sure that Nate is a better and more intelligent boy than he was when he enlisted." Now it was time to "cook my meat and coffee and then go to my hard bed and sleep a little while…good night."[188]

* * *

Always the farmer thinking of home, Nathan wanted to know if "Friend James," the hired hand, had "time this summer [to] get the stumps off" in the old meadow. Lucy wrote that James had thoughts of voting for Vallandigham. Nathan feared that if Ohio elected him, "there will be war there. He is nothing but a traitor in disguise. I would vote for him as soon as I would for Jeff Davis. No, I would not, for I consider the latter the most honorable of the two." He believed that candidates like Vallandigham helped to prolong the war because the southerners hoped such divisive people might lead to a negotiated peace that guaranteed the independence of the Confederacy.

"You are seeing good and easy times, but come here and look," he advised James. "Then go ask that east Tennessee man, and he can tell you more than I can write. Hundreds of them are daily fleeing their homes and joining the Union army." People in the region had been brutally punished for being Unionists. "Hope you will take this advice kindly and write me your opinion on the subject." Nathan heard the local militia was going to march after the picnic on the Fourth of July. "I would like to take a squad and drill them."[189]

The hot Kentucky weather of June continued into July. Nathan had never experienced such temperatures in Ohio. "I think my woolen clothes will almost kill me this summer," he wrote to Lucy. "You know that I sweat very easy, and they being coarse cloth makes me chafe and scratch all the time." Swimming down by the mill creek had helped, but he was back in his "kennel" trying to avoid the sun's heat. "People are in the midst of harvesting here." Farmers were paying a dollar per day to soldiers wanting to earn extra money. He had just finished washing and mending his clothes. "Married women won't have anything to do when they get home." Dinner today included beef, pork, potatoes and pancakes. "We live pretty well today and tomorrow we starve, and so it goes."[190]

The Fourth of July was somewhat cooler. News of the Confederate surrender at Vicksburg and the Union victory at Gettysburg had yet to arrive. "We are going to have an oration at ten o'clock then at five, dress parade." Under orders from General Carter, the regiments under his command were to have a morning prayer and a sermon from the chaplain. The festivities started with the singing of "My Country, 'tis of Thee, Sweet Land of Liberty."[191] However, Nathan's mind was elsewhere, thinking of the holiday picnics back home in Rockport. Yet he did not "have the blues…I feel first rate." The coming of locust in Ohio was being seen locally as a bad sign for the course of the war, but Nathan did not believe it. "Lucy, I am not discouraged in the least about the war but am pleased to think when the Rebs were in Pennsylvania how quick the people turned out. Oh how I wish they would invade Ohio and see whether the people would turn out or let them run over the state."[192]

Veterans of the 103rd Infantry began holding reunions after the Civil War. Annual Camp Weeks in Sheffield Lake continue today for descendants of these veterans. *Courtesy of 103rd OVI Museum.*

The regiment packed up the next morning and headed north for Danville, Kentucky. "It was rumored that the enemy, having crossed the Cumberland River above us, was hoping to catch us napping." Captain Hayes of F Company believed the Rebels were after Union horses and supplies in the Blue Grass country of the state. Passing through Somerset, they heard the news of the Union victory at Gettysburg and the Rebel army's retreat out of Pennsylvania. The force march was hampered by heavy rains and muddy roads and then hot, humid temperatures under a blazing sun. Many soldiers dropped out along the road. They tramped day and night with little rest in between, and some were so exhausted that "the instant we were stopped, they spread out their blankets and lay down for the night without tasting a mouthful of supper."[193]

Near Danville on a Sunday, Nathan started a letter to his wife. "How are those little girls? By this time today, they are at Sunday school." He wanted to know if the Rockport militia under Captain Henry Romp drilled everyday. News from home was scarce. The transportation of mail had been blocked because Morgan was again carrying out raids in Kentucky:

> *One week ago today we started from the Cumberland River, a distance of fifty miles from here. We marched only ten miles yesterday but marched pretty fast. We have had a pretty hard time of it*...[but] *the war news caused a good deal celebrating. Vicksburg is ours, General Lee has been badly whipped. We are anxiously awaiting to hear from General Meade's army and annihilation of the Rebel army in the east.*[194]

A week later and still in the same camp, Nathan's optimism over the recent Union victories had not waned. For the first time since the war began, he saw "a dim light of peace or the prospect of it." However, Morgan was now in southern Ohio. Still angry over Lucy's antiwar neighbors, he wished Morgan "was in Rockport. But do not be alarmed...he will never get there." According to the *Cincinnati Commercial*, the Confederate raiders were "surrounded and would have to fight or surrender." Nathan had heard that Morgan was afraid of the 103rd Infantry, as he always fled from the Ohioans when being pursued in Kentucky. Nevertheless, a Rebel raid into his home state amounted to little in the final outcome of the war because the "Confederacy is cut in twain [and] their armies demoralized."

Nathan believed a negotiated peace to restore the union was now possible—even with the North insisting on the abolition of slavery. "I suppose your father is as much opposed to the war and the way it is carried on as ever he was. Well, he will have to carry it on the same as if he were satisfied with all the proceedings." Lucy had written him about the illness of two elderly neighbors. "The old adage says the old must die. The young may die, but people die everywhere [and] we will all die when our time comes."[195]

A storm swept through Kentucky the following night. Nathan recalled severe weather back home, but this one was "more and heavier thunder. You know very little what thunder is in Ohio. Get in the Cumberland Mountains once if you

After serving in the Union navy, Wilbur Bently volunteered in December 1863 for the 23rd Ohio Infantry. Five months earlier, the regiment had pursued Morgan into Ohio. *Olmsted Historical Society.*

want to hear heavy thunder." Ansel Jordan's health remained precarious. "He is not very well at present...Charley Brown and William Johnson are sick in the hospital but not confined to bed." Willie Romp and his company had gone to Danville for provost duty. They were all enjoying fresh vegetables. "We confiscated a plenty of potatoes." People call the Danville region "the garden of Kentucky."

Since her husband was now a corporal, Lucy thought he had little if any duty. "They have as much responsibility at times as the Captain," Nathan wrote to her. "They have to see that [privates] do their duty and do it properly. They have no duty. Only see that men do it." He was amused by the Home Guard in Rockport and Olmsted, feeling they "won't amount to much. As to D.O. Sweet's command, if I were to give them a name, I should call them the tin copperhead battalion. Wish I were there to make fun of them."[196]

On July 26, Union troopers captured Morgan in southern Ohio. Unaware of the triumph, Nathan read a letter from Lucy. Henry and Sabrina Beach had visited her and paid him a compliment. "Am obliged to them," he wrote back, "but you know them as well as myself. Guess they spread it on pretty thick." Nathan expected to be named color corporal for the company. During a battle, the color sergeant "carries the flag. If he is killed, then the Color Corporals have to pick it up...the flag has to be kept flying and planted six paces in advance of the regiment." He would be in a dangerous place, but "Nate will never run away and leave it if he becomes one."

Nathan had changed his opinion on his regimental commander. Many wondered why the march to Danville was done in such haste. "Finally it leaked out that Col. Casement had bet whiskey with someone that he could march us here by such a time. Some have died since from the effects of it. The Colonel is not liked very much of late." Ironically, Sterling "has changed wonderfully for some reason, and just as the boys began to like him, we had him taken away from us." He was now a member of General Carter's staff. Nathan believed Sterling's transformation occurred because "he had stopped drinking."[197]

* * *

The following Sunday, Nathan wrote his first letter in a week. "Here we are again after a march of 40 miles since last Tuesday. The Rebs have been making quite a raid in Kentucky" capturing Union supply wagons. Before his regiment saw any action, the Union cavalry had gotten to them at Stanford and "took 150 prisoners and three pieces of cannon." They were again back in camp near Danville, and "the weather is extremely hot here. We had a light shower this morning." He hoped Ohio had rain since Lucy wrote of the dry weather. Almost a year in the army, Nathan could only "imagine something of the cares" on the Rockport farm. "But here in the army, one has no cares but to care for himself and musket. Some are too lazy for that." He wanted to "come home in fair time but am afraid not." Nathan thanked her for the money, but he also needed postage stamps, which were not always available in camp.[198]

By the end of the week, Nathan seemed moody and irritable. Lucy had asked what she should send him. "Nothing that I want but tobacco," he replied. "Have always told you that tobacco was the worst article to get here. After this never ask but send tobacco." Albert Dunham of Rockport was about to join the company. "It will be hard for him to come here among well drilled soldiers also not knowing how to soldier." Lucy might want to know what else Dunham would have to learn. "He has to steal and lie when he can do that and not get caught at it." Then Nathan lectured her because she "seemed to be very much discouraged about war matters." She did not understand the enormity and difficulty of the North's task to win the war. "You must remember that we had nothing to commence with in the way of arms, nothing really. Now that the great wheel has begun to move, how easy it is for the right to be victorious." She also worried about foreign governments helping the Confederacy. Nathan responded:

> *There is Russia on very friendly terms with us. She no doubt would have something to say if either France or England should stick their nose in. All I can say is let them come on. A man may as well spend his lifetime in war pursuits and help to establish a government for those that come after him as to follow some occupation that will fret and weary his mind more than this does.*

Overcome with guilt, Nathan wrote, "It is worst for you than me. I can endure hardships…but when I get to thinking of my family and that old father of mine, it makes me feel as if I done something wrong in leaving them." Nevertheless, he preferred being "a volunteer than a drafted man." She had feared that they "had been in a battle. It is not so. The cavalry done all the fighting before we got there." The temperature had cooled after a rainstorm yesterday. He wondered what the weather was like up in Rockport. And his daughters, what were they doing? "Must look out, for Papa will be home one of these days, and when he does come, he wants to find nice behaved little girls."[199]

With a fixed bayonet, Corporal Nathan Hawkins soberly holds his British Enfield rifle. The Union army mostly used U.S. Springfield rifles. *Courtesy of 103rd OVI Museum.*

Nathan stood picket duty over the weekend while the regiment was paid, but Captain Pickands had gotten the money for him. After Sunday dinner, he sat under a maple tree and felt "rather sleepy to write much." He planned to send Lucy only fifteen dollars because of the need for "socks, a handkerchief, tobacco, and lots of little things." Mary Romp, his sister-in-law, had sent him a letter. "She says your father has little to say of late about war matters. They are going to Niagara Falls one of these days."[200]

A week later, with thunderstorms threatening, General Burnside reviewed the army massed outside of Danville. "There are six regiments of infantry [and] five batteries of artillery." Tennessee troops in the Union army had recently returned from Ohio, where they were pursuing Morgan. "Women would bring them oats in their aprons to feed their horses while the children would bring out baskets of provisions." Nathan imagined the Tennesseans in Rockport with his daughters giving them food and "should like to have fared as well." He included in the letter his photograph, which was "rather dark…the flies were so thick, there was not room enough for them to alight only on my face and neck. Do you think a mustache adds to my looks?" The rumor around camp was "a twenty days march from here to Knoxville." Lucy might not hear from him for a while because they would be on the move.[201]

Chapter 4
EASTERN TENNESSEE

The 103rd Infantry was assigned to the 23rd Army Corps, which consisted of twenty thousand men. Burnside's Army of the Ohio took to the road on August 18, 1863. Captain Hayes of F Company believed the "march across the mountains is one that will never be forgotten by anyone who took part in it and shared its toils and suffering." With muskets and backpacks, they traveled on a trail "almost impassible for a footman with any load whatever." Along the way, they built bridges and corduroy roads. "In addition to all this came the labor of assisting the artillery and baggage wagons."[202]

Although exhausted, Nathan had problems sleeping that first night on the road. The day had been "very warm [and] six or eight died of sun stroke" in another regiment. His thoughts again drifted back to his Rockport farm. He wanted Jim to build a shed over the well. "You can buy the poorest pine lumber for that. The shingles will cost the most of anything…[and] about those sheep of mothers, I think Mr. D. is to deliver only 30 sheep." He did not know when Lucy would get the next letter from him.[203]

Six days later, the regiment stopped and waited until the supply wagons crossed the Cumberland River and caught up with the rest of the corps. They were now building roads on the other side of the river. "Our wagon train is eight miles long, so you can imagine how long it takes to get so many wagons over these hills. You may think those hills in Olmsted are hills, but they are little small knolls compared with these." On the horizon, the Cumberland Mountains would be the greater challenge. He looked at the "lofty peaks" and

Cumberland Gap became an important invasion route for both sides during the Civil War. General Grant called it the Gibraltar of America. *Author's Collection.*

believed the crossing of them was going to be "the greatest undertaking of this war—almost equal, if not quite, to Bonaparte crossing the Alps."

Burnside planned to move his army through three mountain passes. The 103rd Infantry would take the middle route through Big Creek Gap, southwest of the Cumberland Gap. "We have two brigades and sixty pieces of cannon making a train of ten miles long." Traveling day and night, they moved slowly in the heat of late summer. "We are all well for a wonder." But a weary Nathan did "not expect to write much until we get to Knoxville." Lucy should look in the newspapers for the "2d Brigade, 3rd Division, 23d Army Corps" to keep up to date on what was happening to him. "Wonder if you have kept all my letters. Hope you have so if I ever get home I can refer to them."[204]

By the middle of September, the regiment made camp outside of Greenville, Tennessee, about sixty miles east of Knoxville. The journey of seventeen days crossing the Cumberland Mountains had been a grueling experience. "Imagine to yourself men tugging away at a canon [and] pushing the gun carriage while the horseman were whipping and spurring their tired steeds until blood ran down their heels in streams. Then imagine how the men were loaded down with sixty rounds of ammunition [and] from six to ten days rations in your knapsack."

The people in eastern Tennessee welcomed them as liberators after being persecuted for their support for the Union. "I have seen women grab our flag, press it to their bosom, kiss it and say God bless the Yankees…while tears would run down their cheeks." Nathan heard about their suffering.

The Advanced Guard depicts Union cavalry attacking Confederate soldiers. The group sculpture is one of four on the Cuyahoga County Soldiers' and Sailors' Monument. *Author's collection.*

"They have been hung, whipped to death, shot and abused in every way." Fearing death for not joining the Rebel army, the men had gone into the mountains, where they stayed for months away from their families. "No one knows how these people have suffered."[205]

The generals expected a fight to capture Knoxville, but the enemy "fled at the approach of our cavalry." Federal troops had marched into the city on the first day of September. "The railroad, leading from Chattanooga into Virginia, was taken possession of by our forces, and the 103rd, with other troops, took the cars and, passing through Knoxville, moved…about nine miles above Greenville."[206]

On September 15, Nathan wrote a letter to Lucy about a harrowing experience while traveling on the train:

> *We were sent from Knoxville up the railroad to relieve the 100th Regiment. They had fought the Rebs two to one a whole day and about 5 o'clock they surrendered, and we did not get there until daylight the next morning and did not know anything about it until some women hollered at us. The train was stopped. They told us the bridge was burnt a little ways ahead of us, so we got off the cars and marched 6 miles when a citizen came and told us that the 100th were all taken prisoners and if we marched a ½ mile farther we would meet the same fate.*[207]

Colonel Casement did not like the idea of falling back—"it was an unnatural and ungodly command." But they retreated to Lick Creek Bridge, a few miles from Greenville, where the regiment remained until September 19. Albert Dunham arrived a few days later. "He wants Jimmy to tell his wife that he is well and alright." Not all of G Company was in camp. "Frank [Campbell] is on the railroad [and] has gone to Knoxville to guard the train through." Everything was okay, but rations were short. At times like these, Nathan yearned for his wife's homemade butter.[208]

The next day, the regiment moved to Henderson and stayed overnight. They were on the road again the following morning. The men were tired and hungry when reaching Jonesboro near midnight. Six hours later, they were on the road again. "Our progress was slow, however, as the enemy, with whom our advance was skirmishing, showed a determination not to fall back any faster than he was obliged to." They pitched their tents for the night outside of Johnson's Station.[209]

The brigade's camp happened to be on the property of a Confederate sympathizer whose farm had been spared by Rebel soldiers. "His orchard was full of apples, his garden abounded in sweet potatoes, cabbages, etc., his fields contained an abundance of corn, his barn-yard was alive with chickens, turkeys and geese, and his stock of pigs was excellent." The word spread rapidly among the hungry men, who looted the farm, burning the "secesh" fence rails to cook their meals.[210]

On September 22, the 103rd Infantry nearly saw action at Blountsville, forty miles northeast of Greenville. "The battle commenced just before sundown with artillery," Nathan wrote Lucy. "General Burnside had posted our Regiment after dark near the enemy works and ordered us to take them by storm, but the enemy left the fort about two o'clock the next morning." Nathan went on a scouting mission with Captain Pickands "expecting every moment to run onto their pickets but as good luck would have and always has it so far we accomplished our mission without injury and returned to post."[211] The Battle of Blountsville, a Union victory, lasted four hours until the Confederates withdrew after being outflanked.

A cousin of Lucy Hawkins, Francis Frost served in the 1st Ohio Light Artillery, which had pursued Morgan's raiders into Ohio during July 1863. *Olmsted Historical Society.*

A week later, the regiment was back at Greenville and still short on rations. Nathan started to have problems with chronic diarrhea, perhaps from eating "apples three days at a time." He did not tell his wife. Flour and some meat were issued, but "the flour we have to hire baked until our money is almost gone. [I] am in hopes we shall draw hard bread soon." And they had only been given coffee once in the last three weeks. "Willie's company is forty miles from here guarding a small town." Albert Dunham suffered from homesickness, and Frank Campbell still served on the train into Knoxville. "We have pretty cold nights here [and] have had one or two frosts already." Nathan remained optimistic about the outcome of the war. "If our army deserted as fast as the Rebels, we would not do so much."[212]

Except from the news in letters, Nathan had little if any knowledge about his friends and relatives who served in other regiments. More than likely, Amelia Ames met Lucy Hawkins occasionally while shopping at Lawrence's general store in Olmsted. They would have exchanged information about their husbands. Nathan had not seen Sam Ames since the latter part of January.

* * *

Farther to the south, the 124th Infantry had also crossed the Cumberland Mountains in late August. "The sight of these mountains is more than I ever saw before," Sam Ames wrote to his wife. "As I set here, I cannot see the top of them. The sight is splendid." He was now serving in the hospital tent with Private Peter Grauel. "I had a horse furnished for myself and had to take care of it with two others belonging to the doctor and major."[213]

Ames's regiment was in the 21st Corps, Army of the Cumberland, commanded by General Rosecrans. The general was consolidating his scattered army as it moved toward Chattanooga, one hundred miles southwest of Knoxville. On September 9, the Federals occupied Chattanooga after General Bragg's Confederate forces evacuated the city. Three days later, the 21st Corps under General Crittenden began to cross the southern Tennessee border. "We are at Gordon and Lee's Mills in Georgia…Not much time for writing, we are on the move nearly all the time—one night we kept right on until morning. It was so dark Gordon Shortlift, ambulance driver, could not see where to drive only as I rode directly in front of his team with a white bag around my shoulders."[214]

In the meantime, General Longstreet reinforced Bragg's Army of the Tennessee with two corps from Virginia. The Confederates now had numerical superiority. Aware of enemy movements in the vicinity of Chattanooga, Rosecrans began to concentrate his forces south of the city. On September 19 and 20, the opposing armies clashed in the Battle of Chickamauga, the bloodiest fought in the western theater of the war. Although suffering fewer casualties, half the Union army fled back to Chattanooga. Not far behind, Rosecrans lost the battle and his command because of incompetence.

General Thomas and his corps saved the army from a greater defeat by covering the retreat until sundown of the second day. Along with other scattered units in the confusion of battle, the 124th Infantry came under the command of Thomas, fighting bravely and holding its position against the determined attacks of Longstreet's seasoned Virginians.

A few days later in Chattanooga, Ames wrote that "Rosey has just past through our regiment, giving great credit to the 124th Ohio. Well he may, for we stood our ground…the balls and shells flew past in all directions. My horse was hit twice but not to hurt him much."[215] Thinking of the Federal defeat, he told his wife to not believe everything she might read in the newspapers about the battle. "But never mind dear Amelia, your Sam is alright so far, and God grant that I may yet get home alright."[216]

Sam Ames's grim face reflects the ordeal of war while serving in a field hospital, tending to the sick and wounded. *Olmsted Historical Society*.

Ames became the cook for the wounded and sick in the hospital tent. "Our old cook was taken prisoner last Sunday [at Chickamauga] but not against his will we think, for he was not a good Union man."[217] Colonel Oliver Payne had been shot in the thigh and sent home. "Great hopes were built on the battle of Chickamauga. There was talk of 'the backbone of the rebellion being broken.' Little did we think at the time that we should be shut up in this same Chattanooga and nearly starved before relief came. The Rebel camp is in sight."[218]

* * *

Nathan's letters to Lucy were now less frequent. She had to rely more on the *Cleveland Morning Leader*, which published articles from a Louisville newspaper:

> *The Journal has received a special from Knoxville considered entirely reliable that Burnside held the country south from Knoxville to Calhoun*

> *on the Tennessee River and Western & Atlantic Railroad…and east of Knoxville as far as Greenville on the East Tennessee and Virginia Railroad. Burnside's right wing is in communication with Rosecrans, and his position is all that could be desired. His army is in the best health and spirits.*[219]

On October 10, Nathan's long-awaited baptism under fire took place at Blue Springs, ten miles northwest of Greenville. Attempting the disruption of the Federal lines of communication, the Confederates had moved a week earlier toward the railroad line at Bulls Gap. Skirmishes followed for a couple of days before Burnside sent reinforcements that included the 103rd Infantry. Arriving on the scene, two companies of the regiment advanced too far. "They came upon a large force of the enemy, which immediately charged our men, capturing several of them and killing and wounding several more." More companies were ordered into action but were then recalled at sunset.[220]

The regiment moved to Bulls Gap for the night and the next day again took the field. "For a time, the fight waxed quite hot, and as we passed through the town, we could hear the booming of cannon and the rattling of musketry. But we were too late. Night came on about the time we arrived at the front, and the firing on both sides ceased." The men slept on their arms that night, expecting another engagement in the morning. But by sunrise, the enemy had fled, and Blue Springs became another Union victory. The Confederates suffered over two hundred casualties and the Union less than half that number.[221]

Nathan wrote Lucy a long letter on October 15 while in camp near Jonesboro about thirty-five miles east of Bulls Gap. Cold weather had arrived, and they were without warm clothing. "The leaves are falling fast and look red and old on the trees. It makes one think how time passes away." Mail delivery had been very slow, and he had just received the first letters from home since leaving Kentucky. Still on duty elsewhere, Frank Campbell and Willie Romp had missed out on the fighting at Blue Springs:

> *Perhaps you would like to know how Nate felt when he heard the canon and musketry. I was just as cool as I am now. When we advanced toward the enemy, a brisk fire was going on. General Burnside sent for our regiment. We doubled quick it for a mile* [and] *took our position, but it was almost dark, so we did not fight any. But the Rebs sent a shell by way of compliment. It burst in the air, however, and no one was hurt. We were in line of battle all night* [and] *nearly froze, expecting a big fight the next day. But the Rebs got up and left in the night. We lost nine men killed and taken prisoners. It*

The Color Guard on the Soldiers' and Sailors' Monument commemorates the 103rd Infantry's heroics during the Battle of Resaca in May 1864. *Author's collection.*

seems like hard business to see the Federal and Rebel soldiers lying about, some dead and some wounded. The most horrible sight was one of our men wounded in the neck. He was walking to the rear, and the blood was running down in front of him. He was covered all over in blood of his own. These things may seem horrible to you, and it is, but soldiers think nothing about it.[222]

On October 14, members of the 103rd Infantry "cast their first vote as soldiers…solidly for John Brough for Governor of Ohio." A day earlier, Ohio voters had elected Brough by a 58 percent margin over Vallandigham. His victory would be greater with the military vote. With Cuyahoga County giving Brough 70 percent of the vote, Rockport and Olmsted's combined return amounted to 63 percent of the balloting. The *Morning Leader* proclaimed, "Thank God for the glad tidings of great joy the telegraph has already sent through the land from the Buckeye State. The hosts of treason and of sin have been overwhelmed and defeated. The Union cause is triumphant, and the county is saved. Amen and amen."[223]

A week later in camp at Stewards Gap, Nathan rejoiced over the election news from Ohio. "We all voted for Mr. Brough thinking him the best man." He had received a letter from Lucy's father "requesting me to cast my vote for Mr. Vallandigham. I could not see it but answered him as respectable as I could." While on picket duty, Nathan's post had been "in front of a secesh house. I went in and had quite a chat with the family." One of them was married to a colonel in the Confederate army. Nathan thought the officer's wife was "the most intelligent individual I have seen since being in the South, but we could not agree on war matters. She was too much of a lady to get mad" at the questions he asked her. "You can image how I appeared in company with ladies after being away from social society so long—and perfect strangers, too."

Nathan was concerned about the supplying of Union troops in eastern Tennessee. Provisions could not be brought through the Cumberland Mountains during wintertime. Rosecrans had to "defeat Bragg's army so as to bring rations from Nashville. If he does not defeat him, we must either suffer for something to eat or climb those awful mountains, for there is not provisions enough to support this army." Although hilly, the region had enough arable land to help feed Lee's Army of Virginia. "Another reason why we should stay here." Farming was different from Rockport. "They run over their land and do not half till it. The women do more work here than the men."

Frustrated with months of conversing by "the medium of the pen," Nathan longed to talk with Lucy "face to face." Then there were the children. His oldest daughter had written him a letter for the first time. "Who would have thought when papa left home that Libbie would learn to write so soon…Well, you done first rate." He expected letters from Carrie and Nettie in the near future. "I want you to be good girls. Be good to mama and obey the teacher…learn your lessons yourself without asking the teacher too much."[224]

* * *

By the end of October, the 103rd Infantry took to the road, marching from Jonesboro. "I heard someone say 'Nate Hawkins, letter for you,' which awakened me from a reverie. Was thinking of home." After the regiment made camp outside of Greenville, Nathan sat by himself and opened the envelope. Lucy had sent him "Nettie's curl of hair" and post stamps. "I think of you and the children very often." He hoped to get a furlough and see them when the regiment camped for the winter. "I have been promoted as Color Corporal. I have no duty to do such as being on picket or camp guard. It is the easiest duty in the regiment but the most dangerous in action." He again wrote about the Battle of Blue Springs:

> *We have at last heard the bursting of shells and the whizzing of bullets. I had to wink as you have seen persons when you were going to throw something at them. When the shells began to burst, they make the most unearthly noise you ever heard when going through the air. The worst of all is to see the dead and wounded, to hear their cries and groans. God deliver me from ever* [again] *witnessing a hard fought battle.*[225]

Frank Campbell continued to guard "the railroad train. It is a good berth." Nathan had not seen Willie Romp for almost two months since B Company camped near Knoxville in the town of Morristown. He remained perturbed over the Copperhead vote in Ohio. "I think more of a Rebel than a Vallandigham man." Even with more Union victories in the coming months, he thought the war could last one more year. On the other hand, the war might end sooner if Congress makes "the poor devils some offer that they will accept, for I think they would accept most any."[226]

In the meantime, Longstreet had started to move his corps northeast from the siege of Chattanooga. Captain Hayes described the reaction of his army commander: "General Burnside at once began to concentrate the various forces, which he had stationed at different places. Hence it was that, on the 3rd of November, an order was received for all the troops in the vicinity of Jonesboro and Greenville to fall back to Knoxville without delay."[227]

Nathan wrote a letter to his wife on the same day that the regiment prepared to move out of camp. "I cannot come home to eat some of that canned fruit, as we hear that Burnside says no winter quarters for this army." They were receiving only half of their normal rations. "I tell you Lucy, we see hard times." But he felt himself hard enough to survive like "these rocks that lay about here [or] would have been dead long ago. Orders have come to get ready to move immediately, so [I] will finish afterward."[228]

Four days later, Nathan finally had the chance to return to his letter. "Well Lucy, how are you this warm and beautiful morning?" Transported by railroad, they were now camped on the outskirts of Knoxville. On the train, he had seen Frank Campbell for the first time in almost two months. "We were very glad to get back here, for we get plenty to eat but not as much we had in Ole Kentucky. Our rations are mostly fresh beef, soft bread and sugar but little coffee. We had issued last night mixed vegetables for making soup." Winter clothes and blankets were drawn by the men, some of which they had to pay for if it exceeded their clothing allowances. "Wish I had my coat that is at home, for the government charges two dollars more for them this year."

Nathan had a talk with some Rebel prisoners who said their armies were just about beaten but that their leaders would continue the war until there was no one left to fight. He believed Congress should try again to negotiate a peace that would secure the Union. If the Confederacy refused, then we "must fight on until the Southern Confederacy is entirely obliterated, until the foe is entirely driven from the earth." Nathan did not particularly want the war to last until the last Confederate soldier died. Antiwar northerners were also at fault. They continued to give hope to the leaders of the South, who thought their opponents would in time grow tired of the bloodshed and demand peace at the expense of the Union. Dissenters were "nothing but cowards." He had seen similar examples in the South. "They are union when union men talk with them and secesh when the Rebels are about."[229]

The regiment camped in a cedar grove near the Holston River. Nathan expected to spend the coming weeks in this pleasant place exchanging letters with his wife. "The Rebels first made their appearance on the south side of the river. We were building log huts for our winter quarters, but we had to leave them and march out to meet the enemy." In support of the 1st Indiana Battery, regiments of Cameron's Brigade, the 103rd Infantry and the 65th Illinois were stationed inside Fort Dickerson, one of four fortifications south of the river. "We drove them back when they crossed the river and joined the main force. We had an artillery skirmish before they left…On come the Rebs when the battery discharged six cannon loaded with grape and canister which made them turn and run. Then they undertook to plant a battery, but our boys gave them a few shells which hoisted them and their horses high in the air."[230]

G and H Companies received an order the following day to move out of Fort Dickerson for skirmish duty near the Maryville Road, which ran south toward the Confederate lines. But the enemy changed tactics, and artillery duels took place north of the river. The men of Cameron's Brigade viewed the spectacle, which was especially impressive at night. The two detached companies were short on rations and needed to forage for food. Under orders not to fire their muskets, they slaughtered razorback hogs using clubs and rocks. Morale was helped with an issue of whiskey and tobacco.[231]

* * *

The siege of Chattanooga continued into late November. "It is rather hard just now to get feed for the horses," Sam Ames wrote. "Gordon Shortliff and I have been a mile from camp all afternoon of this day pulling dead grass and weeds for his [ambulance] team." General Grant had been sent by Lincoln to break the siege. Union troops were arriving from the western and eastern fronts. "Our regiment has gone down the river to help drive the Rebels off Lookout Mountain; 3 [Federal] Brigades met Gen. Hooker… There was hot work for three days and nights with victory on our side."[232]

Ames had stayed in camp cooking for the sick and wounded in the hospital tent. He did have a chance to visit the regiment in the field and "found them in good spirits." The defeat of the Rebels at Lookout Mountain was the beginning of the end of the siege. "We now have the river and will have the railroad through which will make our mail and rations more certain."[233]

The decisive Battle of Chattanooga took place on Sunday, November 25. Most of Bragg's army held the high ground on Missionary Ridge located southeast of the city. Grant ordered General Sherman to attack Bragg's right flank while General Hooker moved on the left flank. Grant told General Thomas, who had replaced Rosecrans, to begin a partial assault in the center to aid the flank attacks. Thomas's army of twenty-three thousand men easily overran the first line of fortifications and then, against orders, stormed up to the top of the ridge, yelling, "Chickamauga!" The Rebel army lost its nerve, broke ranks and fled in confusion.

In General Hazen's brigade, the 124th Infantry had fallen into ranks for the attack near Orchard Knob, where Grant and Thomas stood watching the action. The regiment was in the thick of the fighting at the very center of the frontal assault. On Tuesday, Ames finally had the time to again write home: "We have been very busy since last Sunday, for we had one of the worst battles here. I was not in the fight…I was with Mr. Grauel and the doctor at the field hospital. I am cooking there now for the wounded men. We had one man killed that was John Litchfield. He was all from our company that

Joseph C. Shields recruited volunteers for the 19th Ohio Light Artillery and then served as the battery's captain from July 28, 1862, to September 15, 1864. *Courtesy of Chris Whipple.*

was killed. Company I lost their captain. He was a brave man and a good officer."[234] A detachment of the Union army, including the 124th Infantry, took to the road the next morning "marching on an average of 20 miles a day until we reached Knoxville." Ames was looking forward to again seeing his friends in the 103rd Infantry and the 19th Ohio Battery.[235]

* * *

After a week of indecisive action around Knoxville, General Longstreet began moving artillery across the river onto Cherokee Heights. His intention was to pound the Federal defenses at Fort Sanders, two miles to the north, but General Cameron reacted quickly to counter this new threat. By the dawn of November 25, the 103rd Infantry along with the 65th Illinois Infantry occupied Armstrong's Hill, located across a ten-acre field from the enemy position. The 24th Kentucky Infantry stood behind a ravine between the two regiments and the river. The men had been drenched by a cold rain the night before but now ate a breakfast of cornmeal under a clearing sky. It turned out to be a pleasant morning except for the sporadic sounds of Rebel bullets in the treetops.[236]

Nathan remembered Libbie's birthday, but his thoughts of home were interrupted in the early afternoon by enemy artillery and a Rebel yell. None of the regiment's commissioned officers were present to issue orders, and by the time the regiment had formed a battle line, the Confederates were coming up the hill.[237] "The Rebs made a charge on us expecting to throw us into confusion." Overwhelmed at first, the regiment began to fall back down the other side of the hill. "But we rallied and went into them," driving the enemy onto the field below. After two hours of furious fighting, the brigade drove the Confederates back to Cherokee Heights. Nathan Hawkins wrote:

> *Our regiment lost about sixty killed and wounded...poor Willie Lewis is no more. He was wounded in the knee. The ball entered his knee pan and come out the underside of the curve of his leg. Two more of our company were wounded, J. Spain and J. Truffler. Nate helped to carry the dead and wounded off the field. He hopes never to see another battle...You wanted to know what we done Thanksgiving Day—we fought a battle. It lasted two hours and thirty-five minutes. That is what we had for Supper.*[238]

The men spent the night, once again without campfires, trying to get some sleep on the cold ground of Armstrong's Hill. "Most of the regiment could not sleep at all, and the few who did manage to lose themselves in unconsciousness for a time did so while shivering with the cold." At four

A sculpture on the Soldiers' and Sailors' Monument, *At Short Range* portrays a Confederate attack being repulsed with canister shot. *Author's collection.*

o'clock in the morning, they were ordered with rifles into formation. Captain Hayes of F Company thought it "military nonsense" to have the men standing in the cold darkness for two hours "grasping frosty gun barrels with gloveless hands." Sunrise came without an enemy attack, but the rest of the day was spent building defenses.[239]

On November 29, Longstreet launched an attack on the north side of the river at Fort Sanders. The 103rd Infantry was not involved, but Nathan heard talk of the battle. An artillery captain from Rhode Island "had cut the fuse off shells so all he had to do was to light them and roll them into the ditch. It was a horrid sight the next morning. All along the line, entrenchments were full of their dead and dying." A Confederate captain was one of the fatally wounded "with both legs blown off." The Federals wanted to carry him out on a stretcher, but he refused, preferring to die with his men. "He was good grit."[240]

Longstreet's defeat at Fort Sanders was the decisive battle of the campaign. Federal casualties amounted to about 100, whereas the Rebels lost nearly eight times that number. Longstreet had originally started the siege of Knoxville to keep Union forces away from Chattanooga, where Grant was victorious four days before the attack on Fort Sanders. Longstreet abandoned the campaign on hearing of Sherman's army moving north from Maryville.

On December 7, Burnside's army moved east out of Knoxville pursuing Longstreet. Union troops forded the Holston River and then marched dripping wet in the cold weather along muddy roads. According to Captain Hayes, "the troops were in no condition to march. Half of them were no more than half clad, and all were nearly destitute of shoes. Provisions were limited, and the Commissary could furnish only half rations at most."[241]

Nathan, however, enjoyed "having quite a comfortable time," as he watched G Company leave Knoxville. "I have not been well since we have been in Tennessee [and] have been troubled with a diarrhea more or less all the time. I am not with the Regiment now. There are always some left behind when the Regiment goes on a march, so I staid [*sic*] this time. The Regiment is 16 miles from here at Strawberry Plains building a bridge. You need not worry about me, for I am not seriously ill."[242]

After nearly three weeks of nonstop duty, Nathan could now rest and recuperate. "The siege is over, thank God. Many a good man has fallen, but time still passes." He received four months back pay but was afraid to send any home until "the mail gets regulated once more." Nathan again visited his mother's friend who had a home "splendidly furnished. I like him very much." His thoughts kept going back to friends and family at home before the war. He had not seen any of them for almost a year and a half:

> *When you write about having your Thanksgiving supper…it brings back to my memory the times of years gone by. It made me have a feeling of happy sadness. You remember how the song reads: "Talk not to me of youthful years gone by, for the happiest time for me is yet." Think you my happiest time is yet to come, Lucy…if I am spared to come home to my family again.*[243]

In early December, Lucy had received a letter from her husband's cousin, Caroline Tomlinson. She was concerned about her and Nathan: "I have felt anxious for your sake…to hear something from Nathan since the severe fighting at Knoxville." And she often thought of Lucy and her "little daughters. I know you do well, that nothing you can do will be left undone for their wants. But dear friend, they are to be trained for another world than this." Caroline wrote about her mother becoming "a Christian" and wondered about Nathan's religious beliefs since joining the army. "I have great hope that Nate may find the same support and strength. Camp life has its temptations and trials, too. But 'our Father in Heaven' is as near him then as if he was by your side at home."[244]

* * *

A week before the Christmas of 1863, the weather turned cold at night but stayed mild during the day. Although still in Knoxville, Nathan had been ordered to rejoin his regiment at Strawberry Plains. Frank Campbell again had guard duty on the railroad. Willie Romp remained detached from the regiment at Cumberland Gap. Lucy had told Nathan of "the funerals of Col. Creighton and Crane. It seems hard when men have fought so long, so hard and so well to get killed and their time so near out, too." And his parents were not well. He hoped to see them again, but there was not "much encouragements about furloughs."

The Union campaign in eastern Tennessee, Nathan believed, caused the Confederates to suffer "a good deal for want of provisions as well as ourselves." But he feared the Rebels were now using poisoned bullets. Ansel Jordan had "a very slight wound hardly breaking the skin, but it turned black and blue and was badly swollen…so that goes to show the bullets were not all right." Willie Lewis's wound had been much more serious. "He died the 8th of this month two weeks after he was wounded. Willie was a good soldier [and] was generally liked. There were a good many sick and wounded in the hospital at the time he died, [and] he probably did not receive the proper attention he should have had there." Jacob Spain died of his wounds two weeks later.

William W. Lewis died from wounds on December 21, 1863. His body was later reinterred from Knoxville National Cemetery and buried in Butternut Ridge Cemetery. *Author's collection.*

Nathan purchased food to prepare for his early Christmas supper, which he planned to eat before leaving the next day for Strawberry Plains. He would feast on "potatoes, eggs, sweet potatoes, pie and fresh pork. Well that is good enough for a soldier." Going into his second holiday season away from home, he was trying to make the best of it. "A Merry Christmas to all—also my love to you and the children, father and mother."[245]

As it turned out, Nathan did not leave Knoxville until after Christmas. He spent the holiday with Frank Campbell, and "it was a merry one indeed." He also saw friends from back home, Sam Ames and Andrew Rose.[246] Arriving with the 124th Infantry from Chattanooga, Ames wrote his wife that "Nathan Hawkins and Frank Campbell…were all well and hearty and would be glad to be home, as I would."[247] Within the week, Nathan said goodbye to his Olmsted friends and brother-in-law and rejoined the regiment.

Captain Pickands had been in the Cleveland area signing up recruits. He returned with homemade socks and mittens. "We are the most dirty and ragged looking set of men you ever saw." Nathan was "sorry the Captain did not go out and see the folks and farm," but he did not have the time. Pickands had lost eighty dollars returning to the regiment, and Nathan "let him have forty dollars," so Lucy would be getting "quite a little pile next pay day." It was still not safe to mail any money to her. "Maybe Nate can come and bring it himself."

Listening to the rain dripping on the tent, Nathan told her "it is nothing but mud, mud." Being the last day of the year, he wondered if Lucy had made "any preparations for tomorrow. Only think how soon one year flies away. Two New Year's Days have passed since I have seen you but hope before another year rolls around Nate can take a squint at his little family and their little home." Then darkness closed in on him as he finished the letter. "Libbie must be a good speller as her papa used to be as she leaves off at the head of her class so often. And Carrie, what has become of her? Guess she is the same old six pence full of fun and good heart as ever. Nettie, well she is a stranger, but they tell me she is spunky and fights her way. Well, goodbye old dear family.[248]

The Hawkins daughters appear in this albumen photograph taken in the early 1880s. Carrie, Libbie and Nettie pose from left to right. *Olmsted Historical Society*.

The next morning, Nathan wished his wife a Happy New Year. "No doubt you will be more happy than myself, as you are at home with all the comforts of life and, more particular, have enough to eat and wear." Perhaps he was feeling sorry for himself or simply making her aware of his condition. "We here in the army are suffering with cold and hunger." The first day of the year was bitter cold in the mountains of eastern Tennessee. The men tried to keep warm with campfires outside their pup tents, but they still shivered from the frigid wind. "In speaking of the comforts of life, mankind are apt to complain no matter how well they are situated. I know when we were in Kentucky with plenty to eat and wear we complained. People hardly know when they are well situated but let them come into the army and experience the hardships of a soldiers life then their better judgment will tell them to let well enough alone."[249]

Grant had come north from Chattanooga and arrived in Knoxville. Nathan heard rumors of his regiment becoming part of a sixty thousand-man army that would attack Richmond. "If this move is made, in my opinion, it will be the closing scene of the American rebellion. But it will take some time to accomplish this move."[250]

With the wind, snow and dropping temperatures, Nathan had not been able to finish his letter. Rain had frozen on the tents, several of which had blown down around camp. Besides the shortage of food, many of the men had no overcoats or enough blankets to protect them from the fury of winter. "The country in every direction had been overrun by hungry soldiers of both armies," but their foraging for the most part was unsuccessful. The second day of the year "brought no relief," Hayes recalled. "Both the cold and the scanty fare continued, with this improvement in regard to provisions, that two ounces of meal and a small bit of lean beef were issued to each man."[251]

Nathan went back to his letter to Lucy a few days later. "We have had an awful cold spell…nearly as cold as I ever saw in Ohio." The regiment had been told to pack up and get ready to move at anytime. He had seen "General Grant yesterday. He is rather a rough looking man but seems as though he was clever." Nathan visited with Frank Campbell, who was "enjoying himself quite well I think. Am glad he has an easy berth." Willie Romp and B Company were back with the regiment. "Willie is tough as a knot. He appears contented and happy" earning extra money making finger rings and fixing watches. (After the war, Romp worked at the same vocation.) Nathan ended the letter with a post script: "Tell father if he would write me a letter requesting me to come home, and write in such a way that I could show it to the Captain, maybe that would have some effect. Have him say that we had business to settle of importance, and I can fix the rest."[252]

* * *

The weather turned warmer in the middle of January. Perhaps planning an attack on Knoxville, Longstreet had been concentrating his troops in Dandridge. Intending to counter his movements, Union forces were ordered to engage the Confederate army. "There was nothing particularly remarkable connected with our march to Dandridge," Hayes recalled. "But the retreat from that place was among the most noted events of our whole army life." Longstreet had sent out skirmishers and then feinted an attack on Knoxville to cover his retreat. "Our generals were thoroughly deceived by it, and…at once ordered a retreat, even while Longstreet was moving in the opposite direction." Hayes blamed the retreat that became a rout on the "drunken generals" who relied on rumors instead of factual information.[253]

At first, the retreat had gone slowly for the 103rd Infantry. "John Connally, George Hurd, John Jarrett, Ruphy Rawson, Richard Knowles, Hiram Van Guilder and myself [of H Company] concluded that we would get out of the road and lie down and take a rest. When we awoke, it was daylight, and the command had gone." Since there were still other Federal units in the vicinity, they decided to cook and eat a leisurely breakfast. Later, they found shelter in a schoolhouse when it started to rain. "We began to make preparations to move, and when we got out of the house, the Rebels began to fire on us and ordered us to halt, when I broke and ran up the hill in an opposite direction from them." Charles Lanaghan barely escaped being captured, unlike his less fortunate comrades.[254]

In the confusion of the retreat, Corporal Robert Woodward, George Thorne and William Leggett of G Company were caught behind enemy lines. "After night and darkness came on, we left our hiding place." They planned to sneak by the enemy pickets and rejoin their regiment before the next morning:

> *Our advance in this direction was prevented by a column of Rebel cavalry… guarding a large number of our boys whom they had taken prisoner during the day and who were tramping along, many of them barefoot and coatless, their Rebel captors having taken their coats, boots, and other articles of clothing. We stood behind trees right up to the road, and some of our poor comrades touched the very trees we were hiding behind as they passed, most of them to die in Rebel prisons. The vaunted spirit of Southern chivalry went down below zero, in our estimation at that time, and has never risen since.*[255]

Nearly becoming prisoners themselves, the men were helped by a Unionist farmer who fed them and a soldier from a loyal Tennessee regiment who guided them safely back to Federal lines across Strawberry Plains Bridge. "We found our regiment and received a very kindly welcome from our Captain, H.S. Pickands, and all the boys." A week later, Woodward was promoted to sergeant.[256]

Two weeks later, Lucy Hawkins received a letter from Frank Campbell telling her that Nathan had been taken prisoner. "Oh how bad it made me feel to hear such news. Myself and the children had a loud old cry."[257] Then Captain Pickands confirmed the bad news: "I regret to inform you that your husband, Corporal Nathan W. Hawkins of my Company, has been missing since the 19th day of January." Pickands assumed he had been taken prisoner. "Our Regiment and Brigade was ordered to the front from Dandridge, where heavy skirmishing was taking place with Longstreet's advance." Ansel Jordan and Adam Miller remained behind because of illness, and they "were ordered to remain in camp and only move out in case the wagon train was ordered to the rear. Corporal N.W. Hawkins remained in camp without my knowledge."[258]

Older and a corporal, Nathan may have seen himself as a big brother who needed to take personal care of the helpless privates. Pickands, however, did not hazard a guess. "At 9 o'clock p.m. the [wagon] train was ordered to the rear, and these men with others…were told the army was falling back, but it seems they disregarded the warning and in all probability remained where they were until morning" when the enemy came into Dandridge. The captain had hoped these men would find their way back to the regiment, "but that they were captured is now almost beyond doubt."

Pickands reassured Lucy that her husband "was in excellent health—and much as I regret the unfortunate occurrence, I have no doubts of his final release and return." He had forty dollars that Nathan had given him for safekeeping, which would be sent to her as soon as possible. "I trust you will have full faith in his ultimate (and I hope speedy) release. Any further information that may come to my knowledge I will at once transmit to you—believe me."[259]

Perhaps to lessen the feeling of loss, Lucy felt the need to write her husband, knowing that Pickands would not know where to send the letter. All of her fears went into the letter, as though she were sometimes speaking to herself instead of him: "I fear he is dying of hunger in some dismal prison. Oh how horrible to think of it. If the Rebs used our prisoners as well as we do theirs, they would live on the top shelf. I mean those on Johnson's Island." But she had to talk to him as though Nathan were there ready to answer her letter as he always had since leaving home:

> *To my Dear Absent Husband*
>
> *Dear Nate, it is bedtime, but I am thinking of you. It had not occurred to me that you would be taken prisoner. It seems as if you might starve. You suffered so much at Knoxville, and surely the Rebs must be harder up than our forces if that could be. I do not know if you will ever see this letter, but if you do, you will know that your wife thinks of you. I know if you can write and let me know where you are, you will, and I do hope you will be paroled or exchanged soon.*[260]

While Lucy wrote her letter, Russell Hawkins went to Sunday services at the Congregational church in Rockport. He talked to the Bassetts, who "just had the news of John's death." Private Bassett had died of diphtheria in a hospital at Alexandria, Virginia. His remains arrived in town on Wednesday night for the funeral, which was to be held the following Sunday. They buried him in the Rockport cemetery overlooking the Rocky River Valley, a few miles from the Hawkins farm. Russell's wife could not attend the funeral because she was "very sick with congestion of lungs [and] has a doctor." Lucy planned to attend the Sanitary Fair at a park in Cleveland. "Everyone furnishes something to eat or sell. After the fair is over, the building is to be the soldiers home of Cleveland." She felt "sad and lonely" even when company stayed the night at the farm.[261]

Chapter 5

Home Front

Mistreatment of Union prisoners in the South increasingly alarmed northerners as more reports appeared in local newspapers. Nathan was captured a week before the *Cleveland Leader* published a disturbing article containing a list of over seventy Ohio soldiers who had died over the previous three months at Libby Prison in Richmond, Virginia. Congress responded to the fears of constituents whose relatives were incarcerated by the Confederacy:

> *The Committee on Military Affairs in the House, sometime ago, was instructed to make an examination into reports on the cruelty to our prisoners who are in Rebel hands. The mass of evidence already collected, consisting of affidavits of returned prisoners, statements of officers, etc., are now in the hands of Colonel Deming of Connecticut, there with instructions to continue the investigation and prepare a full report of the same.*[262]

Lucy read the newspapers and worried along with the rest of the Hawkins family. "The barn does not look as if Nate was at home. Guess Nate would not think so himself if he could see it once more." News around Rockport included the death of Libbie Thompson. "How I pity her father and mother. They are so feeble. She has been a good daughter to them." Mr. Silverthorne was "sick with Neuralgia" but was feeling better. Mr. and Mrs. Merwin's daughter, Minnie, was going to have a baby. "Should you thought of it? She

Gravestones for unknown soldiers stand in a prison cemetery at Florence, South Carolina. About 46 percent of Civil War burials in National Cemeteries are unknown. *Author's collection.*

has been with her husband until Christmas." Mag Campbell was worried about Frank since she had not heard from him for a while.[263]

Caroline Tomlinson wrote to her "western cousin," Lucy Hawkins, after hearing Nathan had been taken prisoner. "I do not know what to say now to comfort you when Nathan cannot write to you. Let us hope for the best." She had recently talked to a soldier in Derby, Connecticut. While fighting at Chancellorsville last May, he had been captured and spent four months in Libby Prison on Belle Isle in Richmond. "He said he did not suffer very much…time hung heavy in his hands, and he did not like his food very much, but he did not have to march or fight!"

Another soldier had visited Caroline and told her about living in a rifle pit for eleven days. For over two months, he did not have a tent or a change of clothes. He lost weight but was now forty pounds heavier than he was last September. She closed her letter with religious fervor: "All we can do for Nathan now is to beseech for him the watchful care and protection of God, who is as near to him today as if he were at home with you. In His hands, he is safe. I have strong hope he will be returned to us safe and I hope a Christian Man."[264]

In early spring, Lucy received another letter from Captain Pickands. Writing from Tennessee, he had expected an answer from his February correspondence but had not heard from her. Pickands "had $40 which was due Nathan and until the present time…had no opportunity to send it to you." She should receive the money from the county treasurer in Cleveland. "If you hear from him, I should be glad to know it. Please answer on receipt of this."[265]

Lucy's mother came down from Olmsted Falls and stayed with her in late April. Anna Romp was about to return home when Mag Campbell wrote to her sister wondering if their mother was still at the Rockport farm. "I have again been called to mourn the loss" of yet another loved one. Her mother-in-law had died of typhoid fever. "Won't it be pretty hard for Frank…to hear of two deaths so near to him as his mother and [their daughter] darling little Ida." Mag wanted to know if Lydia Hawkins, Nathan's stepmother, still had myrtle because she wanted to put it "around my dear baby's little bed" in the cemetery. She told Lucy that her "heart aches all the time. It seems sometimes as if it would break." She had to be strong, however, and accept the tragedy as being "all done." Then Mag thought of her missing brother-in-law. "But please don't think I forgot your trouble, for I do not, but think of you so often. Kiss the children for me if you please."[266]

A week later, Lucy received a letter from the Head Quarters Department of Virginia and North Carolina, Officer Commission of Exchange. With the family sitting around her, she nervously opened the envelope. Colonel I.W. Shaffer, chief of staff, acknowledged the letter she sent on April 23: "The Commanding General directs me to inform you that the enclosed letter to your husband was forwarded. Inquiry will be made concerning him by the next Flag of Truce, and all information received will be sent to you."[267]

Mary Romp worried about her sister's apprehension concerning Nathan and compounded with the possibility of the hired hand on the Hawkins farm being drafted: "Jimmie has really got to go, hasn't he? How does he feel about it? Couldn't he get a substitute, or what is the matter? Mr. Weather was here today trying to get some money of Pa. He is going to hire another substitute for his boy and expects it will cost him about $350. I think that is most too bad for poor folks."[268]

* * *

Nathan Hawkins had arrived at Andersonville about the same time in February as John McElroy of the 16th Illinois Cavalry. "About midnight, the train stopped, and we were ordered off.... Stretching out into the darkness was a double row of great heaps of burning pitch pine that smoked and flamed fiercely." McElroy recalled a passage in the *Iliad* of Greek pyres before the walls of Troy. Five hundred prisoners marched between rolls of Rebel guards. "A quarter of a mile from the railroad, we came to a massive palisade of great squared logs standing upright in the ground. The fires blazed up and showed us a section of these, and two massive wooded gates."[269]

Henry Trowbridge from D Company of the 103rd Infantry had been transferred to Andersonville from Libby Prison. "The Andersonville stockade was twenty feet high, the guards standing on the platform on the outside of it. They did not care what went on inside the stockade only so we stayed inside. If the food here was bad, the water was worse. The stream spoken of, which at first had been so beautiful, later became pollution itself."[270]

Trowbridge's first day in the prison began with a sudden awakening. "In the morning after daylight, I felt someone pulling at my knapsack," which he used as a pillow. "I was in a place where the conditions, the need and distress were such that men should be willing to take from another the very necessities of existence." He was soon suffering from "camp diarrhea" because of the water and then a serious cough, which he cured by eating resin from a pine tree. Even if sick, he did not want to be sent to the hospital because "I should certainly have died." Lacking proper treatment and medicine, the hospital was really a death house where few survived.[271]

Prisoners from the same regiments tended to stay together in the same messes. Until coming down with typhoid fever, Nathan Hawkins probably had nominal command over the fifteen privates from the 103rd Infantry. He would have been responsible for dividing up the meager rations, which mostly consisted of coarse ground corn and salted pork. Trowbridge wrote, "At one time, our meat was so lively that it would move itself. We had to boil it in the polluted water, skim the maggots, boil and skim again, and so on until we could manage to eat it and not feel that it was going to crawl when it was down."[272]

In the beginning, the supply of wood inside the stockade was abundant because of the forest debris left over from the construction of the walls. However, by the time of the spring rains, all the wood had been consumed. "The late comers had nothing whatever to build shelter with." The cold rains began in the middle of March and lasted for over two weeks. Those without shelter suffered the most. "The condition of those who had no tents was truly pitiable. They sat or lay on the [muddy] hillside the live-long day and night and took the washing flow with such gloomy composer as they could muster."[273]

April began with warm and sunny weather, but it came too late for many of the prisoners. "The cruel rains had sapped away their stamina…and bore them off at the rate of nearly a score a day." The men were plagued by consumption, bronchitis, pneumonia, dysentery, typhoid fever and, later, scurvy. "It now became a part of the day's regular routine to take a walk past the gates in the morning, inspect and count the dead, and see if any friends were among them." The bodies were nearly naked, having been stripped of all usable garments and shoes. Hands were crossed over the chest and big toes tied together. A scrap of paper contained the soldier's name, rank, company and regiment. "The appearance of the dead was indescribably ghastly. The unclosed eyes shone with a stony glitter."[274]

* * *

Nathan Hawkins wanted to see George Kennedy drafted, but Kennedy managed to stay out of the regular army by volunteering for the 150th Ohio National Guard Regiment. Along with others from Olmsted, Rockport and Dover, he served in I Company. Reverend Jonas Franklin Rice, a Universalist minister, served as the company's first lieutenant. Two days after mustering into service at Camp Cleveland, the regiment departed for Washington on May 7, 1864, to garrison the forts around the city for one hundred days.

With no imminent Confederate attack looming, Kennedy wrote to his wife about coming home on a weekend furlough and seeing "you some Saturday night if I could stay long enough, but to have to come back again would be harder than it was at first. So on the whole, seeing I am weaned, I think of staying the balance of the 100 days before I make a call to you." He joked about not enlisting for three years. "There are some of our boys that are in their element here in the army, and as long there are such fellows, I am willing they should be gratified."

Kennedy believed the regiment was pleased by the "nomination of 'Old Abe' and Andy Johnson." He did not consider himself "a military genius" but felt the war was nearly over. "When I see and hear how things are going on, it seems as if it could not last over this year." Someone had "bet two barrels of beer that Co. I will go home 6 weeks before the rest of the regiment…but I let all such reports go in one ear and right out the other."[275]

Two weeks after leaving Camp Cleveland, Lieutenant Rice wrote a letter to his wife in Olmsted. "I am well, perfectly sound and today am officer of the day at Fort Saratoga. Filled the same position twice last week at Fort Bunker Hill." During one of those days, he had marched his command

Lieutenant Jonas Franklin Rice, a Universalist minister, served in the 150th Infantry, which helped garrison the forts around Washington, D.C., in the summer of 1864. *Olmsted Historical Society.*

past a cemetery, where "over six thousand of our boys sleep...[and] close by it is the soldiers home a place fitted by the government for invalid and destitute soldiers."[276] Lincoln often stayed at the Soldiers Home when he wanted to get away from the White House.

The Confederates unsuccessfully attacked Washington's fortifications starting on July 12. More than likely, soldiers of the 150th Regiment saw Lincoln when he happened to be visiting Fort Stevens during the two-day battle. Rice wrote home the following week:

> *The enemy are far beyond us, and the long lines of armed men who lay in the trenches and rifle pits have all disappeared. Yesterday I visited the battlefield and roamed over it for four or five hours. One of our shells had knocked off a Reb's head. He is* [being] *buried right where he fell. His old hat lies by his side, or at least pieces of it. I took out a piece of lining and rolled up in it a lock of his hair as a memento of the scoundrel's worthless life.*[277]

* * *

Mag Campbell had heard a rumor in Olmsted that Lucy "received a letter from Nate...He had been exchanged and was now with the regiment." In spite of hoping for the best, Mary Romp "did not credit it as we thought if it were so that you would inform us either by coming up or by letter." The sisters had been to Butternut Ridge Cemetery to plant myrtle on Ida's grave but could not "until the grave was fixed. John Ames told me that after dinner he would fix it for me." Mag Campbell had not gotten any news from her husband and was "very anxious to know if there's any foundation" to the rumor about Nathan. "You come up so seldom that we would be glad to hear

John A. Clague fought in the Battle of the Wilderness and died three months later. In 1888, his remains were reinterred in Westlake's Evergreen Cemetery. *Author's collection.*

from you once in awhile anyway." Last week, Mag had received a letter from Willie, who was "well and doing first rate."[278]

William Romp's health was failing, but he did not like wasting money on doctors. On one occasion, his wife had been seriously ill, and a daughter wanted to send for a doctor. Anna Romp did "not consent for fear father would be mad."[279] In the spring, however, he went to see a doctor in Elyria. A week later, Mary Romp believed he was "certainly getting much better…and looks and acts better besides being so cross again as usual—which you know is entirely useless."[280] Diagnosed with inflation of the brain, his condition then worsened, and he died in June. Sabrina Beach attended her brother-in-law's funeral with the rest of the family in the cemetery on Butternut Ridge. She made note of the reading that day from Galatians 6:7: "Be not deceived: God is not mocked. For whatsoever a man soweth, that shall he also reap."[281]

Mourning the loss of her father, Lucy Hawkins still had no idea of the fate of her husband, but news reports were becoming increasingly alarming. A Union soldier had escaped from a prison near Americus, Georgia, which would soon be known in the North as the infamous Andersonville. He told his grim story to his comrades of the 2nd Wisconsin Battery stationed in Chattanooga, Tennessee:

> *The men are without blankets, many of them almost nude, all dirty ragged, dirty and lousy. They have no tents or shelter, except holes they dig in the ground with their hands. Their meat ration is very often minus, and*

> *sometimes their bread and meal; they then get one pint of rice cooked* [per day]. *Two-thirds of the whole 19,000 are suffering from the same dread disease* [scurvy]. *Their limbs are stiff and swollen until they are blue; teeth loose and dropping out, their gums being loose and flappy. The dead are stripped of all clothing, if there be anything but rags on them, and piled into a cart and hauled to the burial ground and there cast into trenches… unshrouded, uncoffined, covered with the cold earth. The mortality is very great. It is to be hoped that some measures may be speedily found to give these men their liberty.*[282]

Lucy may have had some conciliation in Nathan being a prisoner when a Cleveland newspaper listed the casualties of the 103rd Infantry at the Battle of Resaca near Atlanta, Georgia. Among the injured, Albert Dunham of G Company suffered a severe wound to his hip. "Our brigade charged the enemy works," Chaplin Hubbard wrote, "and of course our loss was heavy. We have the proud satisfaction of having carried our flag farthest to the front of any regiment that fought on that day." (*The Color Guard* sculpture on the Soldiers' and Sailors' Monument portrays the mortally wounded color sergeant, Martin Striebler, and eight corporals fighting to protect the regimental flag.) Battlefield deaths included Captain Hutchinson, who led the attack for the absent Colonel Casement, and Captain Philpot of E Company.[283]

As Union forces began the siege of Atlanta, the camps around the beleaguered city became a place of reunions among friends and relatives serving in different regiments. Sam Ames told Amelia that "the Dover boys are all well." He had seen Willie Romp and the other "103rd boys." Ames had gone to see his brother William "and the other boys in the 15th Battery and found them all well and enjoying camp life." William Spafford of Shield's Battery "went down to see them before he came to see me." Serving in A Company of the 1st Ohio Light Artillery, Francis Frost had written Ames from Nashville saying that everything was alright with him and his brother Charles.[284]

* * *

The war came closer to northern Ohio in late September when Confederate agents operating from Canada captured the steamers *Philo Parsons* and *Island Queen* near the Bass Islands of western Lake Erie. Their mission was to free Rebel officers held in the prison on Johnson's Island and burn Sandusky on the other side of the bay. "The capturing party were about thirty with abundance of revolvers and bowie knives." At the time, William McDowell of Rockport was a drummer in the 128th Regiment on Johnson's Island. Six co-plotters living in Sandusky planned to "spike the guns of the Cleveland Battery in camp." After the arrest of a Rebel agent in Sandusky, plans of the conspiracy fell into the hands of the U.S. military. A gunboat went in pursuit of the two steamers. Fleeing across Lake Erie, the Confederates sank the *Island Queen* before abandoning the *Philo Parsons* at Sandwich, Canada.[285]

Daniel Huntington of the 130th Ohio Infantry was taken prisoner when Confederates captured the *Island Queen* in western Lake Erie. After the war, he moved to Olmsted. *Olmsted Historical Society*.

Rumors of more Rebel plots on the shores of the lake continued into October, but the upcoming presidential election dominated the headlines. Township meetings were scheduled throughout Cuyahoga County for supporters of the candidates. Former U.S. Army general George B. McClellan, who had opposed slave emancipation, became the Democratic nominee. Ignoring most of his party's platform, he believed the Union's restoration had to be accepted by the South before any ending of warfare. He hoped to get the vote of all northerners critical of Lincoln's war policies.

In an effort to broaden his political base, Lincoln ran for reelection as a Union Party candidate. Andrew Johnson, a War Democrat from Tennessee, became the vice-presidential nominee. Rockport's meeting for the Union Party took place six days before the election. "Union men, turn out yourselves and see that your neighbors, whether they are Democrats or Union men, are present too."[286]

On that same morning, another disturbing article appeared on the front page of the *Cleveland Leader*:

> *Prisoners who escaped Andersonville say the deaths among Union prisoners at the place averaged about 100 daily during the month of August, principally from scurvy and starvation. After the fall of Atlanta, the Rebels feared raids would be made for the release of prisoner at Macon and other points, and these posts were fortified.*[287]

Ohio congressman James A. Garfield, who had served on Rosecrans's general staff at Chickamauga, arrived in Cleveland on election eve after campaigning for Lincoln in Illinois. "He is looking quite well, notwithstanding his arduous labors." The next day, precautions were taken in the city to prevent "whiskied and bellicose Copperheads and rampart Confederates and Canadian roughs" from disrupting the voting. Police and soldiers patrolled the streets. "The steamer *Michigan* lies quietly down here in the river. A section of artillery is in readiness to speak soothing words to those who may need them." Unionists were encouraged to be vigilant to prevent fraud at the polls. "Copperheads, driven to desperation by the prospect of defeat, will attempt any stratagem to secure a victory. They will attempt illegal voting and violence. Go after breakfast, take your dinner, and stay all day. Create no riot, and allow none. Attempt no illegal voting and allow none."[288]

The next morning, the *Leader* proclaimed: "GLORY HALLEJAH. Clean Sweep of the Free States. All of 'em for Lincoln…Where are you Mac?" Lincoln easily won the balloting in Ohio, but the returns from Rockport were closer, giving the Unionists 170 votes to 132 for the Democrats. In Olmsted, the president received 61 percent of the votes. Even with Union victories in Georgia and Virginia, many voters in the townships had tired of the bloodshed and believed McClellan could end the war earlier than Lincoln.[289]

Lucy Hawkins wondered how the election would affect the fate of her husband. Reports in the newspapers were encouraging. "The long talked of exchange of prisoners at Savannah began on the fifteenth of this month. Ten thousand Rebel prisoners, many of them sick, had arrive…The transfer of Union prisoners was to begin the next day, but the Rebel means of transporting them, both by land and water, being very inadequate, it will take to the first of December." However, there continued to be accounts of "starvation, robbery, neglect, murder, insults worse to bear than even death itself." On the last day of November, the *Cleveland Leader* published a long list of Ohio soldiers from Georgia prisons who had been transported to Annapolis, Maryland, but none of them had served with the 103rd Infantry.[290]

* * *

By Thanksgiving Day 1864, Lucy Hawkins had not seen her husband in over two years nor heard from him in nearly a year. Nevertheless, she was thankful not to have received word of his death. Thinking of the holiday meals before the war, Lucy probably wondered what Nathan was having for dinner. The newspapers had reported the donation of food by eastern cities for the armies of Grant and Sheridan in Virginia: "No soldier's mouth will go unfilled on Thanksgiving Day with the delicious meat, white and brown, of the great American bird, the turkey. Thousands have become a willing sacrifice on the altar of their country, and hereafter let the turkey and the eagle both be mentioned with equal gratitude and reverence."[291]

Even though Lucy did not know for sure where Nathan had been incarcerated, he most likely had been taken to Andersonville. During the weeks before Christmas, rumors of the conditions in the prison were now being confirmed by the ill health of former prisoners hospitalized in Annapolis. Headlines in the *Leader* may have caused Lucy to give up any hope she might still have for his survival:

THE HORRORS OF ANDERSONVILLE
Conditions of the Victims
Their Bones Projecting through the Flesh
Live Men Devoured by Vermin
Skeletons Covered with Withered Skin
Hundreds Brought North Merely to Die[292]

The commander within the prison stockade, Captain Henry Wirz, and "other petty tyrants" were blamed for the suffering of the prisoners who "would like to punish their brute captors. The account given shows that the Rebel officials are responsible, not the Southern people, nor the Southern veteran." A commission was named "to further the ends of truth and justice…into the diabolism of treason."[293] Union soldiers would soon discover outside the stockade the mass graves of some thirteen thousand prisoners.

In the middle of December, an announcement appeared in the newspapers. By flag of truce, the Confederacy would now permit delivery of certain articles for Union prisoners: pants, underclothes, shoes, socks, coats, vests, hats, handkerchiefs, soap, towels, combs, brushes, brooms, lard, sausage, butter, pepper, corn meal, smoked beef, fish, apples, crackers, cheese, mustard, vegetables, dry fruit, sugar, yeast powder, nuts, salt, lemons, nutmeg, matches, tin ware, pocket knives, tobacco, cigars, pipes, snuff, paper, envelopes, steel pens, lead pencils, postage stamps, thread and needles.[294]

During the week before Christmas, a winter storm hit northern Ohio. In Cleveland, "the tracks were so choked up that the streetcars made little headway, and finally stopped." At the Academy of Music, the evening performance of *Aladdin* played to a smaller audience than usual because of the weather. "All should see this spectacular piece at least once." (A year earlier, John Wilkes Booth had played Richard III in the same theatre.[295]) Shopping for "the holidays was never more extensive than now." City stores had "splendid editions of Scott, Prescott, Irving, Shakespeare…and the gayest cigar cases in the world and…Scotch plaids, plush cloaking, scarfs and ties of every color."[296]

Lucy and her daughters traditionally spent Christmas with her Rockport and Olmsted relatives. With several inches of snow on the ground, the sleighing was excellent, recalling a time before the war when Aunt Sabrina and others "all went down to Nathan's for a visit."[297] Lucy would sometimes read his old letters. One in particular mentioned holidays at home. "It brings back to my memory the times of years gone by. It made me have a feeling of happy sadness."[298] On the day after Christmas, the *Leader* published a list of northern Ohio prisoners, including two from the 103rd Infantry, who had been exchanged at Charleston, South Carolina.[299]

On New Year's Day, Frank Campbell and Willie Romp were in Columbia, Tennessee, when a flag was presented to their regiment from the people of Cleveland. "We were proud of the regiment as it marched through the crowds in the streets, waving their last adieus to the brave fellows who were so eager to meet the foe…and prouder of it as from time to time news has come to us of fierce fights." Now in command of the regiment, Colonel Philip C. Hayes accepted the flag. "I have the honor to acknowledge the reception of a most beautiful flag. To the extent of our humble ability, we will protect the flag that you have given us and…return it to you soon with its honor untarnished and undimmed to wave over an undivided country where all will again be prosperous and happy as in former times.[300]

* * *

On January 1, 1865, Amelia Ames wrote, "Last eve the old year 1864 departed into the Kingdom of the past, and now we greet upon this Beautiful Sabbath day the advent of the bright happy New Year 1865…[and] though the air is somewhat chilly, we may pronounce it a lovely winter day."[301] A week earlier, her father had written an obituary for his son in a local newspaper:

> *Death of a Young Soldier*
> *Dover, O. Dec. 23, 1864*
> *Eds. Beacon.—Henry Carroll Merriam, son of E. Merriam of Dover, O. and member of 15th Ohio Battery, died of chronic diarrhea, aged 17 years, 4 months and 24 days. He was sworn in, May 21st, 1864, and was immediately sent to Columbus* [Ohio], *where he was assigned to the 15th Battery and sent right on. He found the battery on the lines June 16th, making its way with Sherman's army to Atlanta, Ga. He was thus initiated into actual service without any previous military experience. The duties were too hard for one so young and slender, and he soon took sick. When they reached Atlanta, he went into the hospital but soon got better and returned to duty, but in a short time was back in the hospital again. From Atlanta, he was sent to Chattanooga, then to Nashville, and then to Evansville, where he died.*
> *E. Merriam*

On the following Sunday, Amelia attended a morning service at the Wesleyan Methodist Church on Lorain Road. (In 2005, the Olmsted Historical Society moved the church to Frostville in the Rocky River Reservation of the Cleveland Metroparks.) Accompanied by her father, she returned to the church for an evening service:

> *I saw sitting directly opposite me a person who reminded me very forcibly of my poor dead brother. We may try and call*

Two months short of his seventeenth birthday, Henry Merriam joined the 15th Light Artillery on May 21, 1864. He died of dysentery in December 1864. *Olmsted Historical Society.*

> *to mind the constancies of our friends by trying to dwell upon the happy hours we spent with them when they were here present with us, but all our efforts amount to almost nothing. There is nothing (at least to my mind) which will so stir up past recollections and so touch the heart wounded by the dart of affliction as such a resemblance to a departed one found in the person of a stranger.*[302]

The 124th Infantry now camped near Huntsville, Alabama, in January. "We had a battle with Hood at Nashville on the 15th and 16th of December in which his army was most successfully routed." Afterward, they had a difficult march in the rain for five days but now were "very comfortable here in Huntsville in our little board houses." There were fireplaces and plenty of wood for fires. "We have a good supply of smoked meat on hand [and] had chicken for dinner and roast turkey two days ago."[303]

Henry Zarley had returned to the regiment. He had been captured in May 1864 and almost died of starvation at Andersonville. Zarley used money hidden in buttons on his uniform to purchase additional food from the guards. "During the hot weather of July and August, he says he has known as many as 200, and some times more, die in one day. He was in a prison yard with 30,000 of our men, and the poor fellows had neither tents or blankets to protect them from the heat of day and cold by night."[304]

Ames must have wondered about the other soldiers from his regiment who had been taken prisoner and probably sent to Andersonville. Unknown to Ames, John Reid of K Company died in June 1864 at the prison. John Gould of Ames's company had been missing in action since the Battle of Chickamauga. He had not seen Nathan Hawkins in a year and hoped his friend still survived somewhere in a Southern prison.[305]

After two weeks of "resting up and getting fat," the men were ordered to pack up for a move out of "our fine winter quarters." They boarded a train and left for Eastport, Mississippi. However, Ames and the others in charge of the horses, mules and wagons remained in camp waiting for the next train. Standing next to one of the wagons in the night, he finished a short letter to Amelia. "The candle is most out, so goodbye and God bless you."[306]

The 124th Infantry did not go to Mississippi but instead returned to Huntsville after a brief stay in Nashville. "We are back in our own camp and well with the exceptions of hard colds, which I think we got by going out of our warm houses and riding on the [train] cars." Ames heard that his wife had diphtheria but was feeling better. "It always does me a great deal of good to hear that you and the rest of my friends are well." While in Nashville, Ames

Amelia and Sam Ames survived the hardships of the war years. From 1866 to 1883, they had four daughters and six sons. *Olmsted Historical Society.*

had attended church for the first time since the previous summer. "An old man but a good man, I think, preached an excellent sermon."

Ames looked forward to the day, seven months in the future, when his three-year enlistment would expire. "It is my prayer," he wrote to his wife and daughter, "that we may all live to meet again. God grant." Since leaving home, Ames had been paid $331.60, of which he sent home $250.00. "Dearest Amelia…unless you see fit for others to know our business, you can keep it to yourself."[307]

Ames read that Lincoln had taken the oath for his second inauguration on March 4. Ten days later, his regiment headed north on a train bound for New Market, Tennessee. They continued the journey on foot to Bulls Gap, marching past Dandridge, where Nathan Hawkins had been taken prisoner a year earlier. While at camp in the mountains, Ames received a letter from Pastor L. Smith of Olmsted: "At the request of your afflicted wife and beloved parents, I write to communicate to you the sad intelligence of the death of your child—Ellen May. She died of Scarlet Fever on the 22nd Inst[ant of March] after a brief sickness—only a few days. May the grace of God be sufficient to sustain you in this trying bereavement."[308]

Amelia's diary reveals a mother who has lost her only child and does not want to remain alone at home next to the cemetery with its unbearable memories. "I did all of the ironing, aired and put away Mamie's things, fixed my own, packed my satchel and after cleansing the rest of the [maple] syrup left home…[and] arrived at the Falls all right. I went up to Mrs. [Mag] Campbells. I shortly received an invitation from her to remain all night, which I accepted with a very good grace. I enjoyed my visit here very much and spent a very quiet and pleasant evening."[309]

The next day, she took the train from Olmsted Falls to the Atlantic and Great Western station near University Heights in Cleveland. "[I] purchased my ticket, and in due time I was safe on board the train and whirling over the road to Cleveland at a rapid rate."[310] She went to see Mrs. Abigail Burrows, who had a boardinghouse on University Street within sight of the Cleveland Institute. (Offering a college preparatory curriculum, the Cleveland Institute was a private coeducational school located in the former building of Cleveland University.) The school overlooked Camp Cleveland. The provost marshal general's office had recently announced that recruits for artillery and cavalry regiments were no longer needed, but the camp remained a busy military base.

Mrs. Burrows's family and her boarders were obviously intent on entertaining Amelia to distract her from thinking about her daughter:

> *In the early part of the afternoon, one of the boarders, Mr. Lemoin, an engineer, suddenly entered the kitchen, where Mrs. Burrows and I were sitting.* [He was] *wearing a false face representing an old man with mustache and beard of white about half a yard long. I was considerably startled at first, but we were all soon laughing heartily at the ridiculous figure he cut in it. "I have a whole suit of old clothes," said Mrs. Burrows, "which would match that completely." Mr. Lemoin caught the idea at once. "Get them tonight and I'll dress up and give the girls a little fright," he said quickly. He warned us all to keep the affair a strict secret, which we promised to do, and I thought no more of it until after supper.*
>
> *The front door bell rang, and Mrs. Burrows answered it and presently returned to inform Abbie and Ella that their presence was desired in the sitting room. They went in but retreated precipitately at the sight of the venerable gentleman. The venerable gentleman followed at a double quick. Abbie turned white, and Ella turned red. Abbie retreated to the buttery and sat down on the sugar box. Ella vanished to some other good place. He wore a swallow-tailed coat of black broadcloth, a long red vest and standing collar* [and] *white linen tights which reached about half way below the knee. To supply the place of stockings which were not, pieces of white flannel were pinned around his ankles. His feet were covered with heavy cowhide shoes, and his head was surmounted with a very good-looking beaver hat. This was quite a masquerade for one evening, and everybody enjoyed it very much.*[311]

Two days later, on a Sunday, Amelia heard Mr. Peck preach at the Cleveland Institute: "Text John 3rd 14th—'And as Moses lifted up the serpent in the wilderness, even so must the Son of man be lifted up.'" In the afternoon, she walked with friends down to the Columbus Street Bridge and saw Catholics leaving a church. "There must have been four or five hundred people, and they poured over the bridge a living stream of humanity for nearly fifteen minutes." On Monday, she visited Mr. Hattersly on Superior Street. "A little before noon, the news came that Richmond was taken, and great was the rejoicing throughout the city. Flags were flung to the breeze, and loud mouthed cannon boomed the joyful news upon thousands of expectant ears while newsboys everywhere shouted that the evening *Herald* [for] 5 cents would tell still more."[312]

* * *

In early March, Lucy Hawkins heard of the death of her cousin, Charles Frost. Serving with Battery E of the 1st Ohio Light Artillery, he had contacted smallpox and died on February 13 in a Nashville hospital. The bad news came in a letter to Aunt Sabrina Beach from his brother, Francis Frost, who served in the same battery. Camped outside of Nashville, Francis was in good health and anxious for the war to end.[313]

Charles Frost served in the 1st Light Artillery. In a Nashville hospital on February 13, 1865, he died at the age of twenty-four from smallpox. *Olmsted Historical Society.*

Near the end of the month, Lucy Hawkins saw in the newspaper another list of paroled prisoners from northern Ohio. Two were from the 103rd Infantry but not G Company. Three others came from Sam Ames's regiment. In the same newspaper, the quartermaster general of Ohio asked the Soldiers Aid Society for help with the released prisoners. "It is unnecessary for us to tell our readers how terribly our poor boys have suffered in Rebel prisons or how great their want. The means of the government for supplying their wants has as yet been inadequate, and the poor fellows have been loud in their complaints."[314]

Typical of the season in Cleveland, the first week of April had "balmy air, high wind, rain, sunshine, blue sky and black clouds." On the Public Square, the apple dealer and organ grinder man had returned. "We have seen knots of children dancing and jumping rope." There had been celebrations with the news of the capture of Richmond: "Rejoicing of the People. Glory Enough for One Day." At the same time, the newspaper included another casualty of the war:

> *Headquarters 103d O.V.I., Kinston, N.C. Wm. Bowler, Esq., Cleveland, Ohio. Dear Sir: It becomes my painful duty to inform you of the death of James F. Scarr, Company B, this regiment. To his relatives and friends at home, we beg to offer our heartfelt sympathy and condolences. H.S.P.* [315]

In anticipation and rumors of Lee's surrender, the students of East Rockport School presented an exhibition that was "spoken of by those who were so fortune as to be present as a very pleasant affair." The program included music, declamations, tableaus and dialogs: "Battle Call, He Died for You, Progress, Women's Rights, The Veteran, I'm Waiting for Thee, Escaping the Draft…."[316]

On Palm Sunday, Lee surrendered his army to Grant. When the news reached Cleveland on Monday morning, "the old Secesh gun on the Public Square" was fired to wake up the sleeping city. People began pouring into the streets celebrating all "the live-long day…old and young, rich and poor." Water Street seemed to be "a continuous bed of May flowers, so numerous were the flags…. At night, the work of jollification carried forward with music and pyrotechnic displays."[317]

On the farm in Rockport, all the celebrating around the township may have been bittersweet for Lucy and her daughters. There was still no word on the fate of Corporal Nathan Hawkins. Everyday, she hoped to find his name under the list of paroled prisoners in the newspaper. Two days before Good Friday, the *Leader* published more names, including five from the 103rd Infantry, but Lucy again searched the list in vain.[318]

Amelia Ames in Olmsted looked forward to the day of her husband's return to his farm on Butternut Ridge Road. "The Ridge people had a jollification this afternoon and evening. The old bell was rung again and again, cannons fired, speeches made…over the late victories." Rain fell the next day when the doctor came to see a member of the family, and

On April 28, 1865, 100,000 mourners stood in a misty rain and waited to view the remains of Abraham Lincoln. *Olmsted Historical Society*.

they heard "the sad news of the death of the President. He was shot by an assassin last night…and died this morning at 7 o'clock and 22 minutes."[319]

On Wednesday of the following week, the Universalist Church of Olmsted held a memorial service for Lincoln. "The church was beautifully decorated with wreaths of evergreen interwoven with black crape." Over one side of the pulpit, a U.S. flag hung with "a large and very lifelike picture of Mr. Lincoln." The church bell rang "at short intervals sometime before the commencement of services." A speaker from Cleveland talked "to us, and despite his highly political speech, there was an air of mournful solemnity [and] over all very fitting to the occasion."[320]

On April 28, Sabrina and Henry Beach were among thousands of people who went to Cleveland to mourn the late president.[321] More than likely, Lucy Hawkins and her daughters accompanied them along with others from Rockport and Olmsted. Sometime around 8:30 a.m., Amelia Ames stood watching the long procession at the corner of Erie (East Ninth) and Euclid Streets:

> *The slow-moving column of soldiers and citizens, the caisson heavily draped, the muffled drums and solemn music of the band, the tolling of bells, the firing of cannon, and the drooping of flags and banners with the misty rain falling softly. The President's remains were conveyed to a*

> *beautiful pavilion which had been erected on the Public Square for the purpose. About eleven o'clock we fell into the citizen's procession and about half part twelve looked upon the still, dead face of Abraham Lincoln.*[322]

Half an hour later, Amelia walked to the home of her friends, Mr. and Mrs. Hattersly, who lived at the foot of Superior Street near John D. Rockefeller's wholesale business. (Rockefeller had hired a substitute to take his place in the Union army.) After dinner, she returned to the Public Square and viewed the late president one last time. On the way back to the Hatterslys, she again passed the Weddell House Hotel, where Lincoln had stayed overnight in February 1861:

> *We all sat up until eleven o'clock at night to see the procession leave. It passed down Superior Street directly by our windows and was another solemn as well as mournful spectacle. The whole street was lit up with torchlights carried by the escort, and as the funeral car passed, we could see it plainly. The rain was falling slowly but heavily, and the mournful music of the band did but add to the sadness in our hearts as we took a last long look at the coffin which contained all that now remains of one whom we so loved to honor. It was a sight grand and at the same time sad, oh so sad and mournful. Long after we had retired to rest, the band in the street filled the air with solemn music, and the muffled drums echoes like death upon our ears.*[323]

* * *

On May 3, Lucy Hawkins finally found out the fate of her husband. A newspaper article in the *Cleveland Leader* entitled "FALLEN HEROES" listed over 350 soldiers from northern Ohio who had died at Andersonville. With a sinking heart, she read, "103rd Infantry—Corporal N. Hawkins [G]; Wm Smith [E]; Geo Hurd [H]; S.J. Harrington [I]; A. Miller [I]; W. Thomas [E]; J. Conway [A]; H. Van Guilder [H]; A. Jordan [G]; F. O'Connor [E]."[324] She was officially notified by the government in a letter dated May 10, 1865.[325] Not being told the cause of his death or other details, Lucy wrote a letter that the hospital directory of the U.S. Sanitary Commission answered at the end of June:

> *We have referred to our records and find the following said items, which are all we have regarding the men you inquired for. There is no way of*

determining what became of articles taken from prisoners. I give you all the information in our possession.

N.W. Hawkins Corporal Co. G. 103rd Ohio died in Prison Hospital at Andersonville Ga. on the 8th of May 1864 of Typhoid Fever and was buried in Grave No. 949.

A. Jordan Co. G. 103rd Ohio died in Prison Hospital at Andersonville Ga. on the 20th of Sept. 1864 of Scorbutus and was buried in Grave No. 9,306.[326]

A week earlier, a train had brought the 103rd Infantry back to Cleveland. One out of every four soldiers did not make it home. The regiment had already been mustered out of service at Raleigh, North Carolina. "The area around Union depot was comfortably full of men and women, young and old. Sisters were there to see brothers, children to see fathers, parents to see their boys, sweethearts and wives to see their own."[327] The scene differed from the cheering in September 1862 when the regiment left the city. The anxious crowd now stood silently as the soldiers climbed down from the freight cars. Sergeant Major Robert Fleury came home as the highest-ranking enlisted soldier in the 103rd Infantry.

In Andersonville National Cemetery, headstones mark the graves of 12,912 prisoners, including 451 unknowns. Nathan Hawkins was the 949th prisoner to die in the prison. *Courtesy of William Stark.*

The regiment cleaned up in a nearby washroom and then marched behind Leland's Band up Water and Superior Streets. Now the cheering started as the soldiers came to the Public

Square and "ground arms and put themselves in readiness for a little declamation." After a lengthy speech, General Casement was honored with a wreath, and Colonel Hayes accepted a bouquet on behalf of the regiment. At the conclusion of the ceremony, the officers and enlisted men "were treated to an excellent dinner, after which they marched over to Camp [Cleveland]. They will be paid off…tomorrow."[328]

In the meantime, Amelia Ames had gone "down to Mrs. Bumps in the afternoon [of June 13] to eat English cherries." She told Amelia that "A and B [Companies] of the 124th OVI were to be in Cleveland that day." Sam Ames arrived home at seven o'clock in the evening. "I slept under my own house roof after two years and ten months of service." Amelia wrote in her diary that night: "Sam is a free man once more. How thankful we should [be] to God for all his mercies."[329]

After the war, Frank and Mag Campbell moved to Hillsdale, Michigan, where a daughter became a teacher. Frank later joined the Grand Army of the Republic. *Olmsted Historical Society.*

Two months later, newspapers across the nation reported on the military trial of Henry Wirz, commander of prisoners at Andersonville. The charges included impairing and injuring the health and destroying the lives of soldiers, subjecting them to torture and great suffering and confining them in unhealthy and unwholesome quarters. In addition, he denied them sufficient food, fresh water or adequate medical treatment, resulting in the death of nearly thirteen thousand prisoners.

The trial lasted sixty-three days, during which hundreds of witnesses gave testimony. The tribunal found Wirz guilty and sentenced him to death by hanging on November 10, 1865. The Wirz trial became significant because of its citing in the trials of war criminals in the twentieth century. Military personnel were now to be held accountable for following orders that resulted in crimes against humanity that violated the rules of war.

* * *

On May 30, 1868, James A. Garfield, Ohio congressman and former commander of the 42nd Ohio Infantry, spoke in Arlington National Cemetery on the first Decoration/Memorial Day. The Grand Army of the Republic had recommended a day of national observance. The graves of Civil War soldiers were to be annually decorated with flowers and flags. Almost 150 years later, the thousands who died in the Civil War continue to be honored along with the veterans of all the nation's wars.

In North Olmsted's Butternut Ridge Cemetery, nine victims of the war are buried: William W. Lewis, Henry Merriam, David Mitchell, Mortimer Paddock, John Reublin, Loring Stearns, Ben Thompson, Curtis Thompson and Davis Webster. Tracy Barnes is remembered with a memorial stone. Coe Ridge Cemetery contains the remains of Bertrand Austin. Olmsted Falls's Chestnut Grove Cemetery includes the graves of John Bradford and Henry Stokes. Three soldiers in Westlake's Evergreen Cemetery died in the war: Sherman Sperry, Christopher Domock and James A. Clague. Fairview Park's Rockport Pioneer Cemetery has six tombstones inscribed with the names of those who gave their lives for the Union: John Andrews, John Bassett, Hoxie Landphair, Hiram Landphair and Nathan Hawkins and Ansel Jordan, who are remembered with memorial stones.

The memorial stone for Nathan Hawkins stands eroding in Fairview Park's Rockport Pioneer Cemetery. Ansel Jorden's stone also marks an empty grave. *Author's collection.*

Lucy Hawkins and her daughters may have gone to Georgia and seen Nathan Hawkins's grave in Andersonville National Cemetery. He had often thought about his daughters' education and their future lives. Libbie Hawkins attended Baldwin College, while Nettie went on to Oberlin College. They never married but lived with their mother on her Rockport farm. After going to Hillsdale College in Michigan, Carrie Hawkins married William M. Bassett of Rockport. Russell was their only child. In 1897, she had a daughter with her second husband, Charles Haynes. They named her Lucy in memory of Carrie's mother, who had died four years earlier.[330]

After Carrie Haynes became a widow, she began teaching at the schoolhouse near her home in Fairview Village. Although too young to be a student, Lucy Haynes went to school with her mother. "I got punished for everything I did and didn't do," she said. And if the students misbehaved, she did not "tell on them."[331] At the age of eight, she received advice from her mother in the form of a poem written in a memory book that echoed the words of Nathan Hawkins in 1862:

Never delay
To do the duty which the hour brings
Whether it be in great or smaller things
For who doth know
What he shall do the coming day?[332]

Notes

Chapter 1

1. Hawkins and McBean Files.
2. Guy R. Wheeler, "Hawkins Family Among Early Rockport Settlers" *The Herald*, (Fairview Park, OH) July 19, 1962.
3. Russell T. Hawkins to Sarah Tomlinson, March 25, 1845.
4. Hawkins file.
5. Jeannette Hawkins as quoted in Goebelt, *Fairview Park*, 42.
6. Johnson, *History of Cuyahoga County*, 506; Goebelt, *Fairview Park*; McBean file.
7. Nathan Hawkins to Lucy Hawkins, December 31, 1863, and September 15, 1863.
8. Nathan Hawkins to Lucy Hawkins, July 2, 1863.
9. Johnson, *History of Cuyahoga County*, 490–91.
10. Sabrina Frost to Jarvis Frost, March 4, 1845.
11. Ibid.
12. Lucy Romp to Sabrina Frost, undated.
13. Diary of Sabrina Frost Beach, April 18, 1853, and July 24, 1853.
14. Stark, *History of the 103rd*.
15. Beach Diary, December 1–3, 1853.
16. Ibid., December 7, 1853.
17. McBean file.
18. Beach Diary, July 2, 1854.
19. Ibid., November 26, 1854, and December 10, 1854.
20. Ibid., February 2, 1855.

21. Ibid., April 3, 1853; April 8, 1855; Apr 16, 1855; April 25, 1855.
22. Peake file.
23. Beach Diary, May 19, 1855.
24. Ibid., July 22–26, 1855.
25. Ibid., July 29–August 4, 1855.
26. Ibid., October 19, 1855; November 22, 1855; December 1, 1855; December 8, 1855.
27. Ibid., December 25, 1855, December 27, 1855.
28. Ibid., January 1, 1856.
29. Ibid., January 8, 1856.
30. Ibid., August 28, 1853.
31. Nathan Hawkins to Lucy Hawkins, April 24, 1863; June 23, 1863; December 16, 1863.
32. Beach Diary, February 1, 1856.
33. Ibid., May 2, 1856, and May 11, 1856.
34. Ibid., June 25, 1856.
35. Ibid., November 20, 1856.
36. Nathan Hawkins to Russell Hawkins, September 24, 1862; Nathan Hawkins to Lucy Hawkins, August 18, 1863.
37. Store Ledger for 1857, Lawrence file.
38. Harriet Tomlinson to Nathan Hawkins, April 4, 1857.
39. Nathan Hawkins to Lucy Hawkins, July 2, 1863.
40. *Morning Leader* (Cleveland), September 11, 1860.
41. Ibid.
42. Ibid.
43. Nelson Diary, September 4, 1860.
44. *Morning Leader*, November 3, 1860.
45. Ibid., November 14, 1860.
46. Nelson Diary, January 4, 1861.
47. Ibid., February 15, 1861.
48. *Plain Dealer* (Cleveland), February 15, 1861.
49. Nelson Diary, April 30, 1861.
50. Hayes, *Journal-History*, 9–10.
51. Goebelt, *Fairview Park*, 22–23.
52. Beach Diary, January 23, 1862; Goebelt, *Fairview Park*, 22–24; Beach Diary, August 12, 1862.
53. Goebelt, *Fairview Park*, 58–59.
54. Nathan Hawkins to Lucy Hawkins, May 17, 1863, and December 16, 1863.
55. Ibid., June 12, 1863, and February 8, 1863.

56. *Morning Leader*, July 22, 1862.
57. Ibid.
58. Hayes, *Journal-History*, 11.
59. *Plain Deale*r, August 13, 1862.
60. Stark, *History of the 103rd*, 12.
61. Federal Census of 1860, Cuyahoga County Public Library website.
62. *Morning Leader*, August 28, 1862.
63. Beach Diary, August 20, 1862.
64. "Our Camp Fire," Ames file.
65. Stark, "Remarks Read On Camp Cleveland."
66. Stark, "Civil War Camps at Cleveland," 34.
67. Stark, *History of the 103rd*, 24–25.
68. Ames file.
69. *Plain Dealer*, August 13, 1862; *Morning Leader*, August 25, 1862.
70. *Morning Leader*, August 28, 1862.
71. Ibid.
72. *Morning Leader*, August 25, 1862.
73. *Plain Dealer*, September 5, 1862.
74. *Morning Leader*, September 4, 1862.
75. *Plain Dealer*, September 4, 1862.
76. "Our Camp Fire."
77. Sam Ames to Amelia Ames, December 11, 1862.
78. "Our Camp Fire."

CHAPTER 2

79. Hayes, *Journal-History*, 13.
80. Stark, *History of the 103rd*, 35.
81. Nathan Hawkins to Lucy Hawkins, September 11, 1862.
82. Nathan Hawkins to Russell Hawkins, September 24, 1862; Nathan Hawkins to Lucy Hawkins, September 16, 1862.
83. Frank Campbell to Lucy Hawkins, September 1862.
84. Nathan Hawkins to Lucy Hawkins, October 5 1862; Wheeler, "Hawkins Family Among Early Rockport Settlers."
85. Nathan Hawkins to Lucy Hawkins, October 5, 1862.
86. Frank Campbell to Lucy Hawkins, September 28, 1862.
87. Nathan Hawkins to Lucy Hawkins, October 9, 1862.

88. Ibid.
89. Nathan Hawkins to Lucy Hawkins, November 9, 1862.
90. Ibid., October 21, 1862.
91. Ibid., October 31, 1862.
92. Ibid., November 2, 1862.
93. Ibid., November 5, 1862.
94. Nathan Hawkins to Russell Hawkins, November 11, 1862.
95. Ibid.
96. Nathan Hawkins to Lucy Hawkins, November 9, 1862.
97. Ibid.
98. Nathan Hawkins to Russell Hawkins, November 11, 1862.
99. Nathan Hawkins to Lucy Hawkins, November 14, 1862.
100. Willie Romp to Lucy Hawkins, November 15, 1862.
101. Nathan Hawkins to Lucy Hawkins, November 16, 1862.
102. Ibid.
103. Ibid.
104. Nathan Hawkins to Lucy Hawkins, November 21, 1862.
105. Ibid.
106. Nathan Hawkins to Lucy Hawkins, November 23, 1862.
107. Ibid.
108. Nathan Hawkins to Lucy Hawkins, November 27, 1862.
109. Ibid., November 29, 1862.
110. Ibid., December 1, 1862.
111. Ibid.
112. Frank Campbell to Lucy Hawkins, December 2, 1862.
113. Nathan Hawkins to Lucy Hawkins, December 5, 1862.
114. Ibid., December 7, 1862.
115. Nathan Hawkins to Russell Hawkins, December 10, 1862.
116. Nathan Hawkins to Lucy Hawkins, December 12, 1862.
117. Ibid., December 19, 1862.
118. Ibid., December 21 and 22, 1862.
119. Ibid., December 25, 1862.
120. Ibid.
121. Ibid., January 1, 1863.
122. Hayes, *Journal-History*, 24.
123. Nathan Hawkins to Lucy Hawkins, January 1, 1863.
124. Hayes, *Journal-History*, 24.
125. Nathan Hawkins to Lucy Hawkins, January 4, 1863.
126. Ibid., January 7, 1863, and January 11, 1863.

127. Ibid., January 18, 1863.
128. Ibid.
129. Ibid., January 22, 1863.
130. Ibid., January 23, 1863.
131. Ibid.
132. Ibid.
133. Willie Romp to Lucy Hawkins, January 27, 1863.
134. Nathan Hawkins to Lydia Hawkins, January 28, 1863.
135. Sam Ames to Amelia Ames, January 21, 1863.
136. "Our Camp Fire."
137. Ibid.
138. Ibid.
139. Nathan Hawkins to Lucy Hawkins, January 30, 1863.
140. Ibid.
141. Ibid.
142. Ibid.
143. Ibid., February 8, 1863.
144. Ibid., February 11, 1863.
145. Ibid., February 13, 1863, and March 23, 1863.
146. Ibid., February 21, 1863, and February 13, 1863.
147. Ibid., February 24, 1863.
148. Ibid., March 3, 1863.
149. Ibid.
150. Ibid., March 7, 1863.
151. Ibid., March 10, 1863.
152. Eli Hawkins to Nathan Hawkins, February 25, 1863.
153. Nathan Hawkins to Lucy Hawkins, March 15, 1863.
154. Ibid., March 23, 1863.
155. Nathan Hawkins to Anna Romp, March 27, 1863.
156. Nathan Hawkins to Lucy Hawkins, March 28, 1863.
157. Ibid., March 30, 1863.
158. Ibid.
159. Ibid., April 2, 1863.
160. Ibid., April 6, 1863; April 10, 1863; April 17, 1863.
161. *Morning Leader*, April 27, 1863.
162. Nathan Hawkins to Lucy Hawkins, April 12, 1863.
163. Ibid., April 17, 1863.
164. Ibid.

CHAPTER 3

165. Hayes, *Journal-History*, 26–27.
166. Frank Campbell to Lucy Hawkins, April 20, 1863.
167. Ibid.; Nathan Hawkins to Lucy Hawkins, April 23, 1863.
168. *Morning Leader*, April 21, 1863.
169. Nathan Hawkins to Lucy Hawkins, April 24, 1863, and April 25, 1863.
170. Willie Romp to Lucy Hawkins, May 15, 1863.
171. Ibid.
172. Nathan Hawkins to Lucy Hawkins, May 12, 1863.
173. Ibid., May 15, 1863.
174. Ibid.
175. Ibid., May 28, 1863.
176. Ibid.
177. Ibid.
178. Frank Campbell to Lucy Hawkins, June 5, 1863.
179. Ibid.
180. Nathan Hawkins to Lucy Hawkins, June 7, 1863.
181. Ibid., June 8, 1863.
182. Ibid., June 10, 1863
183. Ibid., June 18, 1863.
184. Ibid., June 19, 1863.
185. Nathan Hawkins to Russell Hawkins, June 18, 1863.
186. Nathan Hawkins to Lucy Hawkins, June 23, 1863.
187. Willie Romp to Lucy Hawkins, June 26, 1863.
188. Nathan Hawkins to Lucy Hawkins, June 23, 1863.
189. Nathan Hawkins to Friend James, June 28, 1863.
190. Nathan Hawkins to Lucy Hawkins, July 2, 1863
191. Hayes, *Journal-History*, 31.
192. Nathan Hawkins to Lucy Hawkins, July 4, 1863.
193. Hayes, *Journal-History*, 32.
194. Nathan Hawkins to Lucy Hawkins, July 12, 1863.
195. Ibid., July 19, 1863.
196. Ibid., July 21, 1863.
197. Ibid., July 26, 1863.
198. Ibid., August 2, 1863.
199. Ibid., August 7, 1863.
200. Ibid., August 9, 1863.
201. Ibid., August 16, 1863.

CHAPTER 4

202. Hayes, *Journal-History*, 35–36.
203. Nathan Hawkins to Lucy Hawkins, August 18, 1863.
204. Ibid., August 24, 1863.
205. Ibid., September 15, 1863.
206. Hayes, *Journal-History*, 38.
207. Nathan Hawkins to Lucy Hawkins, September 15, 1863.
208. Ibid.
209. Hayes, *Journal-History*, 44–46.
210. Ibid.
211. Nathan Hawkins to Lucy Hawkins, September 29, 1863.
212. Ibid., September 29, 1863.
213. Sam Ames to Amelia Ames, August 29, 1863; "Our Camp Fire."
214. "Our Camp Fire."
215. Sam Ames to Amelia Ames, September 23, 1863.
216. Ibid., September 27, 1863.
217. Ibid.
218. "Our Camp Fire."
219. *Morning Leader*, October 7, 1863.
220. Hayes, *Journal-History*, 49–50.
221. Ibid., 51.
222. Nathan Hawkins to Lucy Hawkins, October 15, 1863.
223. Hayes, *Journal-History*, 52.
224. Nathan Hawkins to Lucy Hawkins, October 21, 1863.
225. Ibid., October 28, 1863.
226. Ibid.
227. Hayes, *Journal-History*, 59.
228. Nathan Hawkins to Lucy Hawkins, November 3, 1863.
229. Ibid., November 7, 1863.
230. Ibid., December 16, 63.
231. Stark, *History of the 103rd*, 188–89.
232. "Our Camp Fire."
233. Ibid.
234. Sam Ames to Amelia Ames, September 27, 1863.
235. "Our Camp Fire."
236. Stark, *History of the 103rd*, 193–94.
237. Ibid., 197; Nathan Hawkins to Lucy Hawkins, December 16, 1863.
238. Ibid.
239. Hayes, *Journal-History*, 67; Stark, *History of the 103rd*, 198.

240. Ibid.
241. Hayes, *Journal-History*, 76.
242. Nathan Hawkins to Lucy Hawkins, December 16, 1863.
243. Ibid.
244. C.S. Tomlinson to Lucy Hawkins, December 12, 1863.
245. Nathan Hawkins to Lucy Hawkins, December 19, 1863.
246. Ibid.
247. Sam Ames to Amelia Ames, December 11, 1863.
248. Nathan Hawkins to Lucy Hawkins, December 31, 1863.
249. Ibid., January 1, 1864.
250. Ibid.
251. Hayes, *Journal-History*, 80–83.
252. Nathan Hawkins to Lucy Hawkins, January 4, 1864.
253. Hayes, *Journal-History*, 83–87.
254. Charles Lanaghan, "Retreat from Dandridge," *Personal Reminiscences and Experiences*, 296–98.
255. Robert Woodward, "Some Things I Heard and Saw in the Army," *Personal Reminiscences and Experiences*, 209.
256. Ibid., 213.
257. Lucy Hawkins to Nathan Hawkins, February 7, 1864.
258. H.S. Pickands to Mrs. N.W. Hawkins, February 1, 1864.
259. Ibid.
260. Lucy Hawkins to Nathan Hawkins, February 7, 1864.
261. Ibid., February 11, 1864.

Chapter 5

262. *Leader* (Cleveland), January 23, 1864, and January 25, 1864.
263. Lucy Hawkins to Nathan Hawkins, February 7, 1864.
264. Caroline Tomlinson to Lucy Hawkins, undated.
265. H.S. Pickands to Mrs. N.W. Hawkins, March 29, 1864.
266. Mag Campbell to Lucy Hawkins, April 28, 1864.
267. I.W. Shaffer to Mrs. Lucy W. Hawkins, May 3, 1864.
268. Mary Romp to Lucy Hawkins, May 22, 1864.
269. McElroy, *Andersonville*, 17.
270. Henry Trowbridge, "Prison Life of Henry Trowbridge of Solon, Ohio." *Personal Reminiscences and Experiences*, 308.
271. Ibid., 308–11.

272. Ibid., 310.
273. McElroy, *Andersonville*, 43.
274. Ibid.
275. G.W. Kennedy to his wife, undated.
276. J.F. Rice to Mrs. Rice, May 24, 1864.
277. Ibid., July 17, 1864.
278. Ibid.; Mag Campbell to Lucy Hawkins, May 23, 1864.
279. Mag Campbell to Sister Lucy, undated.
280. Mary Romp to Lucy Hawkins, May 22, 1864.
281. Beach Diary, June 28, 1864.
282. *Leader*, July 25, 1864.
283. Ibid., May 28, 1864.
284. Sam Ames to Amelia Ames, September 26, 1864.
285. *Leader*, September 21, 1864.
286. Ibid., October 19, 1864.
287. Ibid., November 2, 1864.
288. Ibid.
289. Ibid., November 9, 1864, and November 10, 1864.
290. *Leader*, November 21, 1864; November 30, 1864.
291. Ibid., November 21, 1864.
292. Ibid., December 13, 1864.
293. Ibid.
294. Ibid., December 16, 1864.
295. Ibid., November 23, 1863.
296. Ibid., December 22, 1864.
297. Beach Diary, December 25, 1855, and December 27, 1855.
298. Nathan Hawkins to Lucy Hawkins, December 16, 1863.
299. *Leader*, December 26, 1864.
300. Ibid., January 20, 1865.
301. Ames Diary, January 1, 1865.
302. Ibid., January 8, 1865.
303. "Our Camp Fire."
304. Ibid.
305. www.nps.gov/civilwar/soldiers-and-sailors-database.htm.
306. "Our Camp Fire."; Sam Ames to Amelia Ames, January 31, 1365
307. Sam Ames to Amelia Ames, February 12, 1865
308. L. Smith to Sam Ames, March 24, 1865.
309. Amelia Ames Diary, March 29, 1865.
310. Ibid., March 30, 1865.

311. Ibid.
312. Ibid, April 2, 1865; April 3, 1865.
313. Beach Diary, March 1, 1865.
314. *Leader*, March 25, 1865.
315. Ibid., April 4, 1865; April 7, 1865.
316. Ibid., April 8, 1865.
317. Ibid., April 11, 1865.
318. Ibid., April 12, 1865.
319. Amelia Ames Diary, April 15, 1865.
320. Ibid., April 19, 1865.
321. Beach Diary, April 28, 1865.
322. Ames Diary, April 28, 1865.
323. Ibid.
324. *Leader*, May 3, 1865.
325. Solin Hyer to Mrs. Hawkins, May 10, 1865.
326. H.S. Holbrook to Lucy Hawkins, June 27, 1865.
327. *Leader*, June 20, 1865.
328. Ibid.
329. Ames Diary, June 13, 1865; "Our Camp Fire."
330. Goebelt, *Fairview Park*, 201–02.
331. McBean file.
332. Ibid.

BIBLIOGRAPHY

The Century Illustrated Monthly Magazine 34 (August 1887).

Goebelt, Margaret S. *Fairview Park in Historical Review*. Fairview Park, OH: Fairview Park Historical Society, 1978.

Guinaugh, Sharon, *Come Walk with Me: Exploring Fairview Park—Rockport Cemetery, Cuyahoga County, Ohio*. Franklin, TN: American History Press, 2011.

Hayes, Philip C. *Journal-History of the 103rd Infantry Ohio Volunteer Infantry*. Toledo, OH: Commercial Steam Printing House, 1872.

Holzworth, Walter F. *Historical Story of Olmsted Township*. North Olmsted, OH: Privately published, 1966.

Johnson, Crisfield. *History of Cuyahoga County, Ohio*. Cleveland, OH: D.W. Ensign and Co., 1879.

McElroy, John. *Andersonville: A Story of Rebel Military Prisons*. Edited by Philip Van Doren Stern. Greenwich, CN: Fawcett Publications, 1962.

Members of the 103rd Ohio Volunteer Infantry. *Personal Reminiscences and Experiences*. Oberlin, OH: News Printing Co., 1900.

Stark, William C. "Civil War Camps at Cleveland." *Periodical Journal of the Council on America's Military Past* 12, no. 4 (1983).

———. *History of the 103rd Ohio Volunteer Infantry Regiment, 1862–1865*. Ann Arbor, MI: University Microfilms International, 1987.

———. "Remarks Read on Camp Cleveland, Ohio and the U.S. General Hospital at Cleveland at the Historical Marker Dedication in East Tremont." October 11, 2003.

Olmsted Historical Society Files

Ames, Amelia M. and Samuel H.

Beach, Sabrina (Frost).

Campbell, Margaret (Romp).

Kennedy, George.

Lawrence, Orin.

McBean, Lucy.

Nelson, Newell. *Journal for 1860.*

Peake, Joseph.

Rice, Jonas Franklin.

Whipple, John G., trans. *Civil War Letters Written by Corporal Nathan W. Hawkins and Other Members of the 103rd Ohio Volunteer Infantry*. 1961.

Websites

Civil War Soldiers and Sailors System
www.nps.gov/civilwar/soldiers-and-sailors-database.htm

Cuyahoga County Public Library
www.cuyahogalibrary.org

Cuyahoga County Soldiers' and Sailors' Monument
www.soldiersandsailors.com

Sons of Union Veterans of the Civil War
www.suvcw.org

INDEX

A

B

C

T

U

V

W

Z

About the Author

On February 12, 2013, Dale Thomas signed his book *Lincoln's Old Friends of Menard County, Illinois* at the Lincoln Home in Springfield, Illinois. *Courtesy of Lea Thomas.*

Dale Thomas graduated from Kent State University (BS in social studies and education) and Case Western Reserve University (MA in history). Before retiring, he taught social studies for thirty-one years at Bay High School in Bay Village, Ohio. In addition to serving as a judge for History Day at Case Western Reserve University, he has been an advisor for tours at the Western Reserve Historical Society and historian for the Cleveland Civil War Roundtable.

Thomas is the archivist and vice-president for the Olmsted Historical Society and a member of the North Olmsted Landmarks Commission. He is the author of the books *Images of America: North Olmsted* and *Then & Now: Olmsted*. In 2012, The History Press published his third book, *Lincoln's Old Friends of Menard County, Illinois*.

About the Author

Dale and Lea Thomas have been married for fifty years and have two sons, Scot and Geoff. They live in North Olmsted, Ohio, and volunteer for events held at the Olmsted Historical Society's Frostville Museum in the Rocky River Reservation of the Cleveland Metroparks.